Spanish
for
Real Estate
Agents

by

COMMAND® INC.
SPANISH

~• CONSUMER DIVISION •~

Library of Congress Cataloging-in-Publication Data

Command Spanish®, Inc.
        spanish for real estate agents / by command spanish®, inc.
        ISBN 1-888467-43-6

CONTENTS

AUDIO CD TRACK LIST

Track #	Track Title

Disc One

Disc Two

ACKNOWLEDGEMENTS

Command Spanish, Inc. is indebted to Mrs. Lauree Mills-Mooney for her perseverance and great skill in formatting and word processing the manual. Special thanks are given to Dr. Maryjane Dunn for proofing the manual and to Andrew Schiwetz and Melba Chauvin for engineering the audio accompaniment.

ADVISORS TO THE PROJECT OR SPECIAL THANKS

Command Spanish, Inc. would like to express its appreciation to the following professionals for their great contribution to the successful creation of this manual:

Jody Anderson, Texas Manufactured Housing Association

DeAnn Compton, Century 21 Exclusively

Darleen R. Dale, Coldwell Banker, Don Nance, Inc.

Dolores Fairley, REMAX Real Estate Partners

Jacquelyn Gibson, Coldwell Banker, Donovan Real Estate, Inc.

Judy Ishee-McCrary, Ishee Realty, Inc.

Sonja Shine, Carlson/GMAC Real Estate

Adam Watkins, The DeLois Smith All-Star Team, LLC

LANGUAGE CONSULTANTS

M. Edith González De León, B.A., University of Querétaro, **México**

Karen Murphy, B.A. and B. S., Westfield State College, Massachusetts, **United States**

Lucy Yaneth Solano Acosta, M.A., University of Southern Mississippi, and B.A., National
   University of Colombia, Bogotá, **Colombia**

HOW TO USE THIS MANUAL

Program Description

This manual is the most comprehensive and authoritative work of its kind. It has been carefully researched and documented by language specialists and professionals in the field. This manual can be used effectively, in varying degrees, by people with at least three levels of Spanish language proficiency:

- those with no prior knowledge of Spanish;

- those with some formal training in Spanish; and

- those who are bilingual by family circumstance.

Special Features

- *Generic Spanish* - The Spanish used in this program has been chosen for its wide applicability among many different Hispanic groups. Accordingly, it was field-tested by native Spanish-speaking language specialists from various countries in Latin America.

- *Phonetic Encoding* - For those who have no prior knowledge of Spanish, the program includes a complete and easy-to-use phonetic system of sound approximations to aid in the pronunciation of Spanish items.

- *Work Language* - This program targets the actual language used by a professional in his/her daily work. We have disallowed any extraneous material not directly involved with the specific work world for which this manual was designed. (In other words, we don't teach you how to order tacos in Spanish!)

- *One-Way Communication* - The vast majority of language items found in this manual neither require nor assume an extensive verbal response from the Spanish-speakers. Therefore, there is no need for users to possess extensive listening skills in Spanish.

- *Yes/No and Screen Questions* - On those occasions when a response to a question is required or sought, the correct answer will usually be either "yes" or "no," or an answer that can be somewhat anticipated, such as asking for a telephone number. In the latter case, the response would obviously be a series of numbers. This is called a screen question.

HOW TO USE THIS MANUAL (CONTINUED)

Printed Text

In addition to the section entitled "Spanish Pronunciation," there are 18 chapters devoted to all phases of routine activities performed by real estate agents. These chapters use a language menu format, which is divided into two columns. The first column identifies the English item, the second column provides both the Spanish equivalent and its phonetic approximation. For those with some formal training in Spanish, we suggest that you use the Spanish Version (equivalent), which is found directly to the right of the English item, and relies on standard Spanish pronunciation using the standard print/sound system. For those with no prior knowledge of Spanish, we suggest you use the Phonetic Encoding, which is indented below the Spanish version, and relies on a phonetic approximation using English sounds.

What does ⇧ mean?

When you see this symbol, "⇧", at the end of the phonetic encoding, it is important to remember to inflect up at the end of the line to make sure that the person you are speaking with understands that you have just asked a question. Because of the way Spanish is constructed and to avoid confusion, it is important to inflect up at the end of a question when no question word is present. It is less important to inflect up, when a question word is used.

Compact Discs

Accompanying the printed text are two CDs that contain the recorded version of the printed materials found in the text. You should use these CDs not only when you first master the material, but subsequently as maintenance CDs to maintain your Spanish-speaking skills. Chapters 1-18 on the CDs present the material in paired fashion so that you first hear the English item, followed immediately by the Spanish equivalent.

On tracks 02-04 of CD One, you will find two completely different ways to learn the correct Spanish pronunciation. The first system reviews standard print/sound rules and principles of Spanish pronunciation. If you have previously studied Spanish in high school or college, we suggest you use this approach. The second system presents a simple and highly effective system of phonetic encoding. You read English out loud and Spanish comes out of your mouth!

SPANISH PRONUNCIATION
CD One, Track 02

The Two Systems

There are two different systems one can use to learn near perfect Spanish pronunciation. System #1 utilizes print/sound relationships. System #2 utilizes phonetic encoding. We suggest that you review both systems before making a determination as to which one best suits your needs. Both systems produce good approximations of spoken Spanish. In other words, you will be understood by native speakers, even though you are speaking with an obvious foreign accent. Be sure to speak out loud and forcefully when practicing your Spanish.

System #1: Print/Sound Relationships (see "Spanish Version" in second column of the language menus throughout the manual)
CD One, Track 03

This system is best used by students who have studied some Spanish in high school or college prior to using this manual. This approach involves reading Spanish as if it were English, with the exception of the following consonants, vowels, and rules for stress.

Group A - Pronunciation of Seven Spanish Consonants: g, q, h, j, ll, ñ, rr

1. **G**   g+e and g+i = h as in the English word "hello." Ex: **gente, Gerardo, gitano, giro**

2. **G**   g+a, g+o, and g+u = hard g as in the English word "game." Ex: **ganar, goma, gula**

3. **G**   g+ue = gay as in the English word "gay." Ex: **apague, guerra**
      g+ui = gee as in the English words "geese" or "geezer." Ex: **guiar, guitarra**

4. **Q**   q is always followed by either **ue** or **ui**:
      que= kay as in the English name "Kay." Ex: **quedar, saque**
      qui= key as in the English word "key." Ex: **quién, quitar**

5. **H**   h is always silent. Ex: **hola, hambre, ahora, Hernández**

6. **J**   j = h in English. Ex: **José, baja, ojo**

7. **LL**   ll = y as in the English word "yawn." Ex: **calle, caballo, llorar**

8. **Ñ**   ñ = "ni" as in the English word "onion." Ex: **leña, señor, cañón**

9. **RR**   rr is always trilled. Ex: **carro, burro, torre**
      (All words beginning with "r" are also trilled. Ex: **Roberto, roto, ruido, risa**)

Pronunciation Practice for Consonants

/g/	general, ginebra, ganar, gente, gula, girar, Gabriel, gitano, geografía, seguro
/q/	que, quién, quedar, aquí, quiere, toque, quince, quítese
/h/	hielo, hola, Hernández, honesto, habla, Humberto
/j/	José, Juan, Jesús, jefe, Jalapa, trabaja, juzgado, juicio, abajo
/ll/	caballo, calle, cállese, llano, chillar, llorar, castillo, amarillo, llama
/ñ/	año, leña, Señor, español, cariño, cañón, uña
/rr/	carro, correo, barranca, romper, arriba, Puertorriqueño, rango

SPANISH PRONUNCIATION (CONTINUED)

Group B - Vowels

1. **a** = "**ah**" as in "father." Ex: **casa, loma, alas**

2. **e** = "**ay**" as in "day." Ex: **le, me, celos**

3. **i** = "**ee**" as in "see." Ex: **Lima, fila, institución**

4. **o** = "**oh**" as in "toe." Ex: **oportuno, bola, año**

5. **u** = "**oo**" as in "cool." Ex: **una, mula, usar**

Pronunciation Practice for Vowels

/a/	la, cara, alto, hablar, charlar, malo, águila
/e/	le, echar, comer, esto, merendar, deber
/i/	mi, isla, imitar, pasillo, decir
/o/	lo, como, omitir, hola, pollo, ropa
/u/	un, usar, lumbre, suspiro, estufa

Group C - Vowel Combinations

1. **au** = "**ow**" as in "wow." Ex: **auto**

2. **ia** = "**yah**" as in "yacht." Ex: **licencia**

3. **ie** = "**yay**" as in "yeah." Ex: **tiene**

4. **io** = "**yoh**" as in "yogurt." Ex: **Antonio**

5. **ua** = "**wah**" as in "wander." Ex: **agua**

6. **ui** = "**wee**" as in "weird." Ex: **Luis**

7. **ue** = "**way**" as in "wait." Ex: **luego**

8. **ai** = "**eye**" as in "eyeglasses." Ex: **traigo**

9. **iu** = "**you**" as in "youth." Ex: **ciudad**

10. **ei** = "**ei**" as in "vein." Ex: **treinta**

Pronunciation Practice for Vowel Combinations

/au/	gaucho, auge, ausente, causa, automóvil
/ia/	estudiar, diablo, fianza, liar, enviar, piano
/ie/	pie, tiene, siente, entiende, pierna, viene
/io/	nación, silencio, identificación, estudio
/ua/	paraguas, cual, Juan, suave, acuario
/ui/	Luis, fuiste, cuidado, buitre
/ue/	puede, suelo, mueva, buenos, vuelta
/ai/	caigo, traigo, baile, gaitero
/iu/	ciudadano, diurno, viuda
/ei/	treinta, veinte, seis

Group D - Rules for Spanish Accentuation (stress)

1. Any word ending in a vowel (**a, e, i, o,** or **u**) or **n** or **s**, is stressed on the next-to-the-last syllable.
Ex. ca̱sa, to̱man, etc.
2. Any word ending in any consonant other than **n** or **s** is stressed on the last syllable. Ex. co**mer**.
3. An accent mark overrides rules number 1 & 2. Ex. **Ló**pez, es**tú**pido, etc.

Pronunciation Practice for Accentuation
dentista, heredar, fenómeno, farol, catarro, sorprendente, trombón, nacer

SPANISH PRONUNCIATION (CONTINUED)

System #2: Phonetic Encoding
CD One, Track 04

This system is best used by students who have **no prior knowledge** of Spanish. It involves reading made-up and real English words in ENGLISH, such as these:

bway	dee	kwee	oh	pway
comb	foo	loh	own	sair
cone	gah	may	peck	tor

It's easy! But be careful of these two items: "ay" as in day, and "ow" as in cow. When English is read, Spanish magically comes forth! In order to use System #2 correctly, you need only master the following five simple concepts. Remember, speak English!

1. **Syllable Division**
   Words of more than one syllable are divided by a hyphen (-).
   Examples: ven-gah
                   koh-moh
                   dees-cool-pay-may

2. **Word Separation**
   Words are separated by a slash (/), not hyphens.
   Examples: noh / comb-pren-doh
                   ah-brah / lah / pwair-tah
                   koh-moh / ess-tah

3. **Plus Sign**
   Vowel combinations to be pronounced together are fused with a plus sign (+).
   Examples: day-may / soo / lee-sen-see+ah
                   toh-doh / ess-tah / bee+enn
                   day / may-dee+ah / bwell-tah

4. **Trilled "R"**
   A trilled "r" is marked as a double "rr."
   Examples: sahl-gah / dell / kah-rrow
                   may / goose-tah / ell / ah-rrohs

5. **Capitalized (uppercase) Syllable**
   To indicate that a syllable should be stressed, **CAPITAL LETTERS** are used.
   Examples: ess-TOO-fah
                   TOH-dohs / ess-TAHN
                   lay-VON-tay-say

Pronunciation Practice for Phonetic Encoding

1. kwee-DAH-doh
2. KOH-moh / say / YAH-mah
3. SEE+ENN-tay-say
4. BWAY-nohs / DEE-ahs
5. noh / say / pray-oh-COO-pay
6. DOAN-day / nah-SEE+OH
7. ess / oose-TED / see+oo-dah-DAH-noh
8. TEE+AY-nay / ee-den-tee-fee-kah-SEE+OWN

NOTE: On subsequent pages in this manual you will note that the material is divided into two columns. The scheme is as follows:

First Column = English   Second Column = Spanish Version (for those using System #1)
                                  [Second Column = Phonetic Encoding] (for those using System #2)

Chapter 1:
Greetings and Goodbyes

English	Spanish Version & [Phonetic Encoding]
CD One, Track 06	
1. Mr. **OR** Sir.	Señor. [say-**NYOR**]
2. Mrs. * **OR** Ma'am.	Señora. [say-**NYOH**-rah]
3. Miss.	Señorita. [say-nyoh-**REE**-tah]
4. Good morning.	Buenos días. [**BWAY**-nohs/ **DEE**-ahs]
5. Good afternoon.†	Buenas tardes. [**BWAY**-nahs/ **TAR**-days]
6. Good evening. **OR** Good night.	Buenas noches. [**BWAY**-nahs/ **NOH**-chays]
7. Hello.	Hola. [**OH**-lah]
8. Welcome.	Bienvenido. [bee+enn-vay-**NEE**-doh]
9. How are you?	¿Cómo está? [**KOH**-moh/ ess-**TAH**⇧]
10. Very well.	Muy bien. [**MWEE**/ **BEE+ENN**]
11. Goodbye.	Adiós. [ah-**DEE+OHS**]
12. Until later.	Hasta luego. [**AHS**-tah/ **LWAY**-goh]
13. Until tomorrow.	Hasta mañana. [**AHS**-tah/ mah-**NYAH**-nah]

[handwritten] GRACIAS Y USTED = FINE THANX AND YOU

[handwritten] HASTA LA VISTA : Until I see you AGAIN

[handwritten] MAS O MENOS = MORE OR LESS /REGULAR

---

* *If you are not sure whether or not a woman is married, you should address her as "señorita," in spite of her age.*

† *In Latin America, the afternoon may extend to as late as 7:00PM, if there is still some daylight left.*

Chapter 2:
Etiquette and Introductions

English	Spanish Version & [Phonetic Encoding]

CD One, Track 07

1. Yes.

Sí.
[**SEE**]

2. No.

No.
[**NOH**]

3. Excuse me. (when leaving a group, or the table, or making your way through a crowd)

Con permiso.
[cone/ pair-**MEE**-soh]

4. Excuse me. (when bumping into someone)

Perdón.
[pair-**DOHN**]

5. Please.*

Por favor.
[por/ fah-**VOR**]

6. Thank you.

Gracias.
[**GRAH**-see+ahs]

7. You're welcome.

De nada.
[day/ **NAH**-dah]

8. Allow me.

Permítame.
[pair-**MEE**-tah-may]

9. Okay.

Está bien.
[ess-**TAH**/ **BEE+ENN**]

10. I am *(name)*.

Yo· Soy *(name)*.
[**SOY**/ ___]

11. Nice to meet you.

Mucho gusto.
[**MOO**-choh/ **GOOSE**-toh]

Es un placer· ITS A pleaser · encantado

12. The pleasure is mine.

El gusto es mío.
[ell/ **GOOSE**-toh/ **ESS**/ **MEE**-oh]

---

* *Latino culture is etiquette driven. Do not be afraid to sprinkle your conversation with "pleases" and "thank yous."*

Chapter 3:
Communication Strategies

English	Spanish Version & [Phonetic Encoding]

CD One, Track 08

1. Just a moment.

Un momento. *Por Favor (Please)*
[oon/ moh-**MEN**-toh]

2. Do you speak English?

¿Habla inglés?
[**AH**-blah/ een-**GLAYS**♀]

3. Can you respond to questions in English?

¿Puede contestar preguntas en inglés?
[**PWAY**-day/ cone-tays-**TAR**/ pray-**GOON**-tahs/ enn/ een-**GLAYS**♀]

4. I don't speak (much) Spanish.

I'm learning Spanish

No hablo (mucho) español.
[**NOH**/ **AH**-bloh/ (**MOO**-choh)/ ess-pah-**NYOHL**]
Estoy Aprendiendo Espanol

5. I'll try to help you.

Voy a tratar de ayudarle.
[**VOY**/ ah/ trah-**TAR**/ day/ ah-you-**DAR**-lay]

6. I don't understand.

I don't understand

No entiendo.
[**NOH**/ enn-**TEE+ENN**-doh]
No Comprendo.

7. Just tell me yes or no.

Diga "sí" o "no".
[**DEE**-gah/ **SEE**/ oh/ **NOH**]

8. Speak slower.

Hable más despacio.
[**AH**-blay/ **MAHS**/ days-**PAH**-see+oh]

9. Repeat it.

Repítalo.
[rray-**PEE**-tah-loh]

10. Do you understand me?

¿Me entiende?
[may/ enn-**TEE+ENN**-day♀]
Me Comprende? Do you understand me.

11. Do you know how to read in Spanish?

¿Sabe leer en español?
[**SAH**-bay/ lay-**AIR**/ enn/ ess-pah-**NYOHL**♀]

12. Do you know how to read in English?

¿Sabe leer en inglés?
[**SAH**-bay/ lay-**AIR**/ enn/ een-**GLAYS**♀]

13. Read this. (point)

Lea esto. *(Point out)*
[**LAY**-ah/ **ESS**-toh]

14. Do you know how to write in Spanish?

¿Sabe escribir en español?
[**SAH**-bay/ ess-kree-**BEER**/ enn/ ess-pah-**NYOHL**♀]

despacio Por Favor: Slow please
Repita Por Favor: Repeat Please

Chapter 3:
Communication Strategies (cont.)

English	Spanish Version & [Phonetic Encoding]
15. Do you know how to write in English?	¿Sabe escribir en inglés? [**SAH**-bay/ ess-kree-**BEER**/ enn/ een-**GLAYS**♀]
16. Write it here. (point)	Escríbalo aquí. [ess-**KREE**-bah-loh/ ah-**KEY**]
17. Write your name here. (point)	Escriba su nombre aquí. [ess-**KREE**-bah/ soo /**NOME**-bray/ ah-**KEY**]
18. Sign here.* (point)	Firme aquí. [**FEAR**-may/ ah-**KEY**]
19. Do you need an interpreter?	¿Necesita traductor? [nay-say-**SEE**-tah/ trah-duke-**TOR**♀]
20. Do you know someone who can help you as an interpreter?	¿Conoce a alguien que le pueda ayudar como traductor? [koh-**NOH**-say/ ah/ **AHL**-ghee+enn/ kay/ lay/ **PWAY**-dah/ ah-you-**DAR**/ **KOH**-moh/ trah-duke-**TOR**♀]
21. Respond in English, if possible.	Responda en inglés, si es posible. [rrays-**POHN**-dah/ enn/ een-**GLAYS**/ see/ **ESS**/ poh-**SEE**-blay]
22. Letter by letter.†	Letra por letra. [**LAY**-trah/ por/ **LAY**-trah]
23. Number by number.‡	Número por número. [**NOO**-may-roh/ por/ **NOO**-may-roh]

* See "Appendix A: Cultural Notes" on page 63.
† See "Apendix B: Spanish Alphabet" on page 64.
‡ See Chapter 4, "Numbers" on page 7.

Chapter 4:
Numbers

English	Spanish Version & [Phonetic Encoding]

CD One, Track 09

0. zero — cero
[**SAY**-roh]

1. one — uno
[**OO**-noh]

2. two — dos
[**DOHS**]

3. three — tres
[**TRACE**]

4. four — cuatro
[**KWAH**-troh]

5. five — cinco
[**SEEN**-koh]

6. six — seis
[**SACE**]

7. seven — siete
[**SEE+AY**-tay]

8. eight — ocho
[**OH**-choh]

9. nine — nueve
[**NWAY**-vay]

10. ten — diez
[**DEE+ACE**]

11. eleven — once
[**OHN**-say]

12. twelve — doce
[**DOH**-say]

13. thirteen — trece
[**TRAY**-say]

14. fourteen — catorce
[kah-**TOR**-say]

15. fifteen — quince
[**KEEN**-say]

16. sixteen — dieciséis
[dee+ay-see-**SACE**]

17. seventeen — diecisiete
[dee+ay-see-**SEE+AY**-tay]

18. eighteen — dieciocho
[dee+ay-**SEE+OH**-choh]

19. nineteen — diecinueve
[dee+ay-see-**NWAY**-vay]

20. twenty — veinte
[**VAIN**-tay]

21. twenty-one — veintiuno
[vain-**TEE+OO**-noh]

Chapter 4:
Numbers (cont.)

English	Spanish Version & [Phonetic Encoding]
22. twenty-two	veintidós [vain-tee-**DOHS**]
23. twenty-three	veintitrés [vain-tee-**TRACE**]
24. twenty-four	veinticuatro [vain-tee-**KWAH**-troh]
25. twenty-five	veinticinco [vain-tee-**SEEN**-koh]
26. twenty-six	veintiséis [vain-tee-**SACE**]
27. twenty-seven	veintisiete [vain-tee-**SEE+AY**-tay]
28. twenty-eight	veintiocho [vain-**TEE+OH**-choh]
29. twenty-nine	veintinueve [vain-tee-**NWAY**-vay]
30. thirty	treinta [**TRAIN**-tah]
31. thirty-one	treinta y uno [**TRAIN**-tah/ ee/ **OO**-noh]
32. thirty-two (etc. etc.)*	treinta y dos [**TRAIN**-tah/ ee/ **DOHS**]
40. forty	cuarenta [kwah-**REN**-tah]
50. fifty	cincuenta [seen-**KWEN**-tah]
60. sixty	sesenta [say-**SEN**-tah]
70. seventy	setenta [say-**TEN**-tah]
80. eighty	ochenta [oh-**CHEN**-tah]
90. ninety	noventa [noh-**VENN**-tah]
100. one hundred	cien [**SEE+ENN**]
101. one hundred one	ciento uno [**SEE+ENN**-toh/ **OO**-noh]
102. one hundred two (etc. etc. etc.)†	ciento dos [**SEE+ENN**-toh/ **DOHS**]

---

* *To count from 31-99, link two digit numbers and one digit numbers with the word "**y**", which means "**and**."*

† *To count from 101 to 199, use the word "**ciento**", which means "**one hundred plus**" followed by one or two digit numbers.*

Chapter 4:
Numbers (cont.)

English	Spanish Version & [Phonetic Encoding]
200. two hundred*	doscientos [dohs-**SEE+ENN**-tohs]
300. three hundred	trescientos [trace-**SEE+ENN**-tohs]
400. four hundred	cuatrocientos [kwah-troh-**SEE+ENN**-tohs]
500. five hundred	quinientos [kee-**NEE+ENN**-tohs]
600. six hundred	seiscientos [sace-**SEE+ENN**-tohs]
700. seven hundred	setecientos [say-tay-**SEE+ENN**-tohs]
800. eight hundred	ochocientos [oh-choh-**SEE+ENN**-tohs]
900. nine hundred	novecientos [noh-vay-**SEE+ENN**-tohs]
1,000. one thousand†	mil [**MEEL**]
1,001. one thousand one	mil uno [**MEEL/ OO**-noh]
1,002. one thousand two (etc. etc. etc.)‡	mil dos [**MEEL/ DOHS**]
2,000. two thousand (etc. etc. etc.)§	dos mil [**DOHS/ MEEL**]
10,000. ten thousand (etc. etc. etc.)	diez mil [**DEE+ACE/ MEEL**]
50,000. fifty thousand (etc. etc. etc.)	cincuenta mil [seen-**KWEN**-tah/ **MEEL**]
100,000. one hundred thousand (etc. etc. etc.)	cien mil [**SEE+ENN/ MEEL**]
120,000. one hundred twenty thousand (etc. etc.)	ciento veinte mil [**SEE+ENN**-toh/ **VAIN**-tay/ **MEEL**]

1,000,000   un million

---

* *To count from 201 to 999, put one or two digit numbers after the "hundreds" word.*

† *Some Spanish-Speaking countries use a comma to denote decimal points and periods to show thousands.*

‡ *To count from 1001 to 1,999, use the word "**mil**", which means "**one thousand**" followed by one, two or three digit numbers.*

§ *About numbers from 2,001 to 999,999, use one, two, or three digit numbers followed by "**mil**", which means "**thousand**"; then add one, two or three digit numbers.*

Chapter 5:
Receiving Customers and Prospects

English	Spanish Version & [Phonetic Encoding]
CD One, Track 10	

1. Come in.

Pase.
[**PAH**-say]

2. May I help you?

¿En qué puedo ayudarle?
[enn/ **KAY**/ **PWAY**-doh/ ah-you-**DAR**-lay☺]

3. Do you have an appointment?

¿Tiene una cita?
[**TEE+AY**-nay/ **OO**-nah/ **SEE**-tah☺]

4. With whom?

¿Con quién?
[cone/ **KEE+ENN**☺]

5. With whom would you like to speak?

¿Con quién desea hablar?
[cone/ **KEE+ENN**/ day-**SAY**-ah/ ah-**BLAHR**☺]

6. Would you like to speak with an agent?

¿Desea hablar con un agente de bienes raíces?*
[day-**SAY**-ah/ ah-**BLAHR**/ cone/ oon/ ah-**HEN**-tay/ day/ **BEE+AY**-nays/ rrah-**EE**-says☺]

7. What's your/his/her (complete) name?†

¿Cuál es su nombre (completo)?
[**KWAHL**/ **ESS**/ soo/ **NOME**-bray/ (comb-**PLAY**-toh)☺]

8. Sit down.

Siéntese.
[**SEE+ENN**-tay-say]

9. Wait here.

Espere aquí.
[ess-**PAY**-ray/ ah-**KEE**]

10. An agent will be with you soon.

Un agente viene a ayudarle pronto.
[oon/ ah-**HEN**-tay/ **VEE+AY**-nay/ ah/ ah-you-**DAR**-lay/ **PRONE**-toh]

---

* *See "Appendix A: Cultural Notes" on page 63.*
† *See "Appendix C: Spanish Surname System" on page 65.*

Chapter 6:
Interview for Housing Needs and Preferences

English	Spanish Version & [Phonetic Encoding]

Unit A: Customer's Realty and Personal Information
CD One, Track 11

1. Let's begin.

Empecemos.
[emm-pay-**SAY**-mohs]

2. Let me ask you a couple of questions first.

Permítame hacerle unas preguntas primero.
[pair-**MEE**-tah-may/ ah-**SAIR**-lay/ **OO**-nahs/ pray-**GOON**-tahs/ pree-**MAY**-roh]

3. Are you already working with a realtor?

¿Ya tiene agente de bienes raíces?
[**YAH**/ **TEE+AY**-nay/ ah-**HEN**-tay/ day/ **BEE+AY**-nays/ rrah-**EE**-says♀]

4. Do you have a contract with that realtor?

¿Tiene un contrato con ese agente?
[**TEE+AY**-nay/ oon/ cone-**TRAH**-toh/ cone/ **AY**-say/ ah-**HEN**-tay♀]

5. You have to work with your realtor.

Tiene que seguir con ese agente.
[**TEE+AY**-nay/ kay/ say-**GEAR**/ cone/ **AY**-say/ ah-**HEN**-tay]

6. We can be your realtor.

Podemos ser su agente de bienes raíces.
[poh-**DAY**-mohs/ **SAIR**/ soo/ ah-**HEN**-tay/ day/ **BEE+AY**-nays/ rrah-**EE**-says]

7. In what city do you live now?

¿En qué ciudad vive ahora?
[enn/ **KAY**/ see+oo-**DAHD**/ **VEE**-vay/ ah-**OH**-rah♀]

8. What's your address?

¿Cuál es su dirección?
[**KWAHL**/ **ESS**/ soo/ dee-rex-**SEE+OHN**♀]

9. What is the best phone number to reach you at?

¿Cuál es el mejor número de teléfono para llamarle?
[**KWAHL**/ **ESS**/ ell/ may-**HOHR**/ **NOO**-may-roh/ day/ tay-**LAY**-foh-noh/ **PAH**-rah/ yah-**MAHR**-lay♀]

10. What's your email address?

¿Cuál es su dirección de correo electrónico?
[**KWAHL**/ **ESS**/ soo/ dee-rex-**SEE+OHN**/ day/ koh-**RRAY**-oh/ ay-leck-**TROH**-nee-koh♀]

11. Where do you work?

¿Dónde trabaja?
[**DOAN**-day/ trah-**BAH**-hah♀]

Chapter 6:
Interview for Housing Needs and Preferences (cont.)

English	Spanish Version & [Phonetic Encoding]

Unit B: Customer's Financial Information
CD One, Track 12

1. Is this your first home purchase in the U.S.?

   ¿Es la primera vez que compra vivienda en los Estados Unidos?
   [**ESS**/ lah/ pree-**MAY**-rah/ **VACE**/ kay/ **COMB**-prah/ vee-**VEE+ENN**-dah/ enn/ lohs/ ess-**TAH**-dohs/ oo-**NEE**-dohs ☝]

2. Have you selected a lender to provide a loan?*

   ¿Ya escogió un banco o un prestamista para el préstamo?
   [**YAH**/ ess-koh-**HEE+OH**/ oon/ **BAHN**-koh/ oh/ oon/ prays-tah-**MEES**-tah/ **PAH**-rah/ ell/ **PRAYS**-tah-moh ☝]

3. Have you been prequalified by a bank or a lending institution?

   ¿Ya pre-calificó para un préstamo con un banco o un prestamista?
   [**YAH**/ pray-kah-lee-fee-**KOH**/ **PAH**-rah/ oon/ **PRAYS**-tah-moh/ cone/ oon/ **BAHN**-koh/ oh/ oon/ prays-tah-**MEES**-tah ☝]

4. Which bank or mortgage company?

   ¿Qué banco o prestamista?
   [**KAY**/ **BAHN**-koh/ oh/ prays-tah-**MEES**-tah ☝]

5. For how much?

   ¿Cuánto le aprobaron?
   [**KWAN**-toh/ lay/ ah-proh-**BAH**-rohn ☝]

6. How much are you willing to spend on a property?

   ¿Cuánto está dispuesto a gastar por una propiedad?
   [**KWAN**-toh/ ess-**TAH**/ dees-**PWAYS**-toh/ ah/ pah-**GAR**/ por/ **OO**-nah/ proh-pee+ay-**DAHD** ☝]

7. How much money are you willing to spend per month?

   ¿Cuánto está dispuesto a pagar al mes?
   [**KWAN**-toh/ ess-**TAH**/ dees-**PWAYS**-toh/ ah/ pah-**GAR**/ ahl/ **MACE** ☝]

Unit C: Customer's Search Options
CD One, Track 13

1. Have you seen any properties you like?

   ¿Ha visto alguna propiedad que le guste?
   [**AH**/ **VEES**-toh/ ahl-**GOO**-nah/ proh-pee+ay-**DAHD**/ kay/ lay/ **GOOSE**-tay ☝]

2. These are for sale on the market. (point to magazine/brochure)

   Estas están a la venta.
   [**ESS**-tahs/ ess-**TAHN**/ ah/ lah/ **VENN**-tah]

3. Let me know if you see anything you like.

   Dígame si ve alguna que le interese.
   [**DEE**-gah-may/ see/ **VAY**/ ahl-**GOO**-nah/ kay/ lay/ een-tay-**RAY**-say]

---

* *See also Chapter 7, "Financial Issues" on page 21.*

Chapter 6:
Interview for Housing Needs and Preferences (cont.)

English	Spanish Version & [Phonetic Encoding]

Unit C: Customer's Search Options (cont.)

4. We can also do a computer search.

También podemos buscar en internet.
[tahm-**BEE+ENN**/ poh-**DAY**-mohs/ boos-**CAR**/ enn/ een-tair-**NET**]

5. We can look for the features you would like.

Podemos buscar las características que usted desea.
[poh-**DAY**-mohs/ boos-**CAR**/ loh/ kay/ oose-**TED**/ day-**SAY**-ah]

6. We can see what's currently available.

Podemos ver lo que está disponible.
[poh-**DAY**-mohs/ **VAIR**/ loh/ kay/ ess-**TAH**/ dees-poh-**NEE**-blay]

7. Would you like me to do a computer search?

¿Desea que busque en la computadora?
[day-**SAY**-ah/ kay/ **BOOS**-kay/ enn/ lah/ comb-poo-tah-**DOH**-rah⇑]

8. I can:

Puedo:
[**PWAY**-doh]

<u>OR</u>

I cannot:

<u>OR</u>

No puedo:
[**NOH**/ **PWAY**-doh]

- do it right now.

- hacerlo ahora mismo.
  [ah-**SAIR**-loh/ ah-**OH**-rah/ **MEES**-moh]

- do it later.

- hacerlo más tarde.
  [ah-**SAIR**-loh/ **MAHS**/ **TAR**-day]

- do the search with you.

- buscar con usted.
  [boos-**CAR**/ cone/ oose-**TED**]

- print the listings for you.

- imprimirle una lista de propiedades.
  [eem-pree-**MEER**-lay/ **OO**-nah/ **LEES**-tah/ day/ proh-pee+ay-**DAH**-days]

- call you about the listings.

- llamarle cuando tenga una lista de propiedades.
  [yah-**MAR**-lay/ **KWAN**-doh/ **TEN**-gah/ **OO**-nah/ **LEES**-tah/ day/ proh-pee+ay-**DAH**-days]

- email you the listings.

- enviarle la lista por correo electrónico.
  [enn-**VEE+ARE**-lay/ lah/ **LEES**-tah/ por/ koh-**RRAY**-oh/ ay-leck-**TROH**-nee-koh]

- mail you the listings.

- enviarle la lista por correo.
  [enn-**VEE+ARE**-lay/ lah/ **LEES**-tah/ por/ koh-**RRAY**-oh]

- show you the pictures.

- mostrarle las fotos.
  [mohs-**TRAHR**-lay/ lahs/ **FOH**-tohs]

Chapter 6:
Interview for Housing Needs and Preferences (cont.)

English	Spanish Version & [Phonetic Encoding]

Unit C: Customer's Search Options (cont.)

8. I can: (cont.)

OR

I cannot:

• give you more information.

• take you to see them.

Puedo:
[**PWAY**-doh]

OR

No puedo:
[**NOH**/ **PWAY**-doh]

• darle más información.
[**DAR**-lay/ **MAHS**/ een-for-mah-**SEE+OHN**]

• llevarle para que las vea.
[yay-**VAHR**-lay/ **PAH**-rah/ kay/ lahs/ **VAY**-ah]

9. Point to the ones you like the most.

Señale las que más le interesan.
[say-**NYAH**-lay/ lahs/ kay/ **MAHS**/ lay/ een-tay-**RAY**-sahn]

Unit D: Customer's Wish List
CD One, Track 14

1. Are you looking for:

OR

Do you have:

OR

Do you live in:

• a house?

• a mobile home?

• a lot?

• land?

¿Está buscando:
[ess-**TAH**/ boos-**KAHN**-doh☺]

OR

¿Tiene:
[**TEE+AY**-nay]

OR

¿Vive en:
[**VEE**-vay/ enn]

• una casa?*
[**OO**-nah/ **KAH**-sah☺]

• una casa móvil?
[**OO**-nah/ **KAH**-sah/ **MOH**-veel☺]

• un lote?
[oon/ **LOH**-tay☺]

• un terreno?
[oon/ tay-**RRAY**-noh☺]

2. Do you own it?

¿Es suya la propiedad?
[**ESS**/ **SOO**-yah/ lah/ proh-pee+ay-**DAHD**☺]

3. Do you pay rent?

¿Paga renta?
[**PAH**-gah/ **RREN**-tah☺]

* *See "Appendix A: Cultural Notes" on page 63.*

Chapter 6:
Interview for Housing Needs and Preferences (cont.)

English	Spanish Version & [Phonetic Encoding]

Unit D: Customer's Wish List (cont.)

4. How many people live there?

¿Cuántas personas viven ahí?
[**KWAN**-tahs/ per-**SOH**-nahs/ **VEE**-venn/ ah-**EE**☞]

5. How many kids live there?

¿Cuántos niños viven ahí?
[**KWAN**-tohs/ **NEE**-nyohs/ **VEE**-venn/ ah-**EE**☞]

6. What age?

¿De qué edad?
[day/ **KAY**/ ay-**DAHD**☞]

7. Would you/he/she like to:

¿Desea:
[day-**SAY**-ah]

   • buy?

   • comprar?
   [comb-**PRAHR**☞]

   • rent?

   • rentar?*
   [rren-**TAR**☞]

   • do that in (#) months?

   • hacerlo en (#) meses?†
   [ah-**SAIR**-loh/ enn/ ___/ **MAY**-says☞]

   • do it sooner than that?

   • hacerlo más pronto?
   [ah-**SAIR**-loh/ **MAHS**/ **PRONE**-toh☞]

8. For rental properties, you can call (# or name).

Para rentar, llame a (# or name).
[**PAH**-rah/ ren-**TAHR**/ **YAH**-may/ ah/ ___]

9. How many people will be living there?

¿Cuántas personas van a vivir ahí?
[**KWAHN**-tahs/ pair-**SOH**-nahs/ **VAHN**/ ah/ vee-**VEER**/ ah-**EE**☞]

10. Fill out this checklist with the things you would like. (give checklist in Spanish)‡

Llene este formulario con las características que usted desea.
[**YAY**-nay/ **ESS**-tay/ for-moo-**LAH**-ree+oh/ cone/ lahs/ kah-rahk-tay-**REES**-tee-kahs/ kay/ oose-**TED**/ day-**SAY**-ah]

11. Does it matter if it's older or newer?

¿Importa si es vieja o nueva?
[eem-**POR**-tah/ see/ **ESS**/ **VEE+AY**-hah/ oh/ **NWAY**-vah☞]

12. How many bedrooms?

¿Cuántas recámaras?
[KWAN-tahs/ rray-**KAH**-mah-rahs☞]

13. How many stories?

¿Cuántos pisos?§
[**KWAN**-tohs/ **PEE**-sohs☞]

---

* See "Appendix A: Cultural Notes" on page 63.

† See Chapter 4, "Numbers" on page 7.

‡ See "Appendix H: Property Features Checklist" on page 73.

§ See "Appendix A: Cultural Notes" on page 63.

Chapter 6:
Interview for Housing Needs and Preferences (cont.)

English	Spanish Version & [Phonetic Encoding]

Unit D: Customer's Wish List (cont.)

14. How many bathrooms?

¿Cuántos baños?
[**KWAN**-tohs/ **BAH**-nyohs☿]

15. Would you/he/she/ like:

¿Desea:
[day-**SAY**-ah]

- a 1-car garage?

• un garaje para un auto?
[oon/ gah-**RAH**-hay/ **PAH**-rah/ oon/ **OW**-toh☿]

- a 2-car garage?

• un garaje para dos autos?
[oon/ gah-**RAH**-hay/ **PAH**-rah/ **DOHS**/ **OW**-tohs☿]

- a carport?

• una cochera?
[**OO**-nah/ koh-**CHAY**-rah☿]

- a dining room?

• un comedor?
[oon/ koh-may-**DOHR**☿]

- a fireplace?

• una chimenea?
[**OO**-nah/ chee-may-**NAY**-ah☿]

- central air conditioner?

•aire acondicionado central?
[**EYE**-ray/ ah-cone-dee-see+oh-**NAH**-doh/ sen-**TRAHL**☿]

- central heat?

• calefacción central?
[kah-lay-fax-**SEE+OHN**/ sen-**TRAHL**☿]

- a basement?

• un sótano?
[oon/ **SOH**-tah-noh☿]

- a big kitchen?

• una cocina grande?
[**OO**-nah/ koh-**SEE**-nah/ **GRAHN**-day☿]

- a fenced yard?

• un jardín cercado?
[oon/ hard-**DEEN**/ sair-**KAH**-doh☿]

16. What city would you/he/she prefer?

¿En qué ciudad desea vivir?
[enn/ **KAY**/ see+oo-**DAHD**/ day-**SAY**-ah/ vee-**VEER**☿]

17. Any area in particular there?

¿En alguna zona en particular ahí?
[enn/ ahl-**GOO**-nah/ **SOH**-nah/ enn/ par-tee-koo-**LAHR**/ ah-**EE**☿]

18. Would you/he/she like to live near:

¿Desea vivir cerca de:
[day-**SAY**-ah/ vee-**VEER**/ **SAIR**-kah/ day]

- a school?

• una escuela?
[**OO**-nah/ ess-**KWAY**-lah☿]

- a mall?

• un centro comercial?
[oon/ **SEN**-troh/ koh-mair-**SEE+AHL**☿]

- a highway?

• una carretera?
[**OO**-nah/ kah-rray-**TAY**-rah☿]

- a store?

• una tienda?
[**OO**-nah/ **TEE+ENN**-dah☿]

Chapter 6:
Interview for Housing Needs and Preferences (cont.)

English	Spanish Version & [Phonetic Encoding]

Unit D: Customer's Wish List (cont.)

18. Would you/he/she like to live near: (cont.)

¿Desea vivir cerca de:
[day-**SAY**-ah/ vee-**VEER**/ **SAIR**-kah/ day]

    • a park?

    • un parque?
      [oon/ **PAR**-kay♙]

    • a bus stop?

    • una parada de autobuses?
      [**OO**-nah/ pah-**RAH**-dah/ day/ ow-toh-**BOO**-says♙]

    • a subway stop?

    • una parada del metro?
      [**OO**-nah/ pah-**RAH**-dah/ dell/ **MAY**-troh♙]

19. Which one?

¿De cuál?
[day/ **KWAHL**♙]

Chapter 7:
Financial Issues

English	Spanish Version & [Phonetic Encoding]

CD One, Track 15

1. We have financing available.
Nosotros hacemos préstamos.
[noh-**SOH**-trohs/ ah-**SAY**-mohs/ **PRAYS**-tah-mohs]

2. Are you interested in a (#) year loan?
¿Le interesa un préstamo a (#) años?*
[lay/ een-tay-**RAY**-sah/ oon/ **PRAYS**-tah-moh/ ah/ ___/ **AH**-nyohs☝]

3. Let me suggest a couple of mortgage companies.
Puedo sugerirle varias compañías que hacen préstamos para vivienda.
[**PWAY**-doh/ soo-hay-**REAR**-lay/ **VAH**-ree+ahs/ comb-pah-**NYEE**-ahs/ kay/ **AH**-sen/ **PRAYS**-tah-mohs/ **PAH**-rah/ vee-**VEE+ENN**-dah]

4. I can arrange an appointment for you with them.
Puedo sacarle una cita con ellos.
[**PWAY**-doh/ sah-**CAR**-lay/ **OO**-nah/ **SEE**-tah/ cone/ **AY**-yohs]

5. This company: (point to card or name)
Esta compañía:
[**ESS**-tah/ comb-pah-**NYEE**-ah]

OR

This bank: (point to card or name)
Este banco:
[**ESS**-tay/ **BAHN**-koh]

• can help you with the loan.
• puede ayudarle con el préstamo.
[**PWAY**-day/ ah-you-**DAR**-lay/ cone/ ell/ **PRAYS**-tah-moh]

• will give you good service.
• presta un buen servicio.
[**PRAYS**-tah/ oon/ **BWAIN**/ sair-**VEE**-see+oh]

• is trustworthy.
• es confiable.
[**ESS**/ cone-**FEE+AH**-blay]

6. They will guarantee:
Ellos garantizan:
[**AY**-yohs/ gah-rahn-**TEE**-sahn]

• the lowest interest rate.
• el interés más bajo.
[ell/ een-tay-**RAYS**/ **MAHS**/ **BAH**-hoh]

• to close on time.
• hacer el cierre a tiempo.
[ah-**SAIR**/ ell/ **SEE+AY**-rray/ ah/ **TEE+EMM**-poh]

• same day approval.
• aprobación el mismo día.
[ah-proh-bah-**SEE+OHN**/ ell/ **MEES**-moh/ **DEE**-ah]

See Chapter 4, "Numbers" on page 7.

Chapter 7:
Financial Issues (cont.)

English	Spanish Version & [Phonetic Encoding]
6. They will guarantee: (cont.)	Ellos garantizan: [**AY**-yohs/ gah-rahn-**TEE**-sahn]
• fixed rates.	• interés fijo. [een-tay-**RAYS**/ **FEE**-hoh]
• adjustable rates.	• interés ajustable. [een-tay-**RAYS**/ ah-hoos-**TAH**-blay]
7. They will:	Van a: [**VAHN**/ ah]
• ask you for your social security number.	• pedirle su número de seguro social. [pay-**DEER**-lay/ soo/ **NOO**-may-roh/ day/ say-**GOO**-roh/ soh-**SEE**+**AHL**]
• request immigration status documents from you.	• pedirle documentos de su estado de inmigración. [pay-**DEER**-lay/ doh-koo-**MEN**-tohs/ day/ soo/ ess-**TAH**-doh/ day/ een-mee-grah-**SEE**+**OHN**]
• require income information from you.	• pedirle información de sus ingresos. [pay-**DEER**-lay/ een-for-mah-**SEE**+**OHN**/ day/ soos/ een-**GRAY**-sohs]
• conduct a credit check on you.	• revisar su historia de crédito. [rray-vee-**SAR**/ soo/ ees-**TOH**-ree+ah/ day/ **KRAY**-dee-toh]
• give you a prequalification letter if everything is OK.	• darle una carta de pre-calificación si todo está bien. [**DAR**-lay/ **OO**-nah/ **CAR**-tah/ day/ pray-kah-lee-fee-kah-**SEE**+**OHN**/ see/ **TOH**-doh/ ess-**TAH**/ **BEE**+**ENN**]
8. The letter will allow you to:	La carta va a permitirle: [lah/ **CAR**-tah/ **VAH**/ ah/ pair-mee-**TEER**-lay]
• see how much you can borrow.	• ver cuánto puede pedir prestado. [**VAIR**/ **KWAN**-toh/ **PWAY**-day/ pay-**DEER**/ prays-**TAH**-doh]
• negotiate the price.	• negociar el precio. [nay-goh-**SEE**+**ARE**/ ell/ **PRAY**-see+oh]
• review properties you know you can afford.	• visitar propiedades que sabe que puede pagar. [vee-see-**TAHR**/ proh-pee+ay-**DAH**-days/ kay/ **SAH**-bay/ kay/ **PWAY**-day/ pah-**GAHR**]
• save time by not looking in price ranges that you cannot afford.	• ahorrar tiempo al no mirar propiedades de precios que no puede pagar. [ah-oh-**RRAHR**/ **TEE**+**EMM**-poh/ ahl/ **NOH**/ mee-**RAHR**/ proh-pee+ay-dah-days/ day/ **PRAY**-see+ohs/ kay/ **NOH**/ **PWAY**-day/ pah-**GAHR**]
• choose the right property for you.	• escoger bien su propiedad. [ess-koh-**HAIR**/ **BEE**+**ENN**/ soo/ proh-pee+ay-**DAHD**]

Chapter 8:
Follow-up Interview After Prequalification

English	Spanish Version & [Phonetic Encoding]

Unit A: Fine-Tuning the Price Range Based on the Prequalification
CD One, Track 16

1. I'm sorry.

Lo siento.
[loh/ **SEE+ENN**-toh]

2. We haven't found anything in your price range.

No hemos encontrado nada de ese precio.
[**NOH**/ **AY**-mohs/ enn-cone-**TRAH**-doh/ **NAH**-dah/ day/ **AY**-say/ **PRAY**-see+oh]

3. Don't be discouraged.

No se desanime.
[**NOH**/ say/ days-ah-**NEE**-may]

4. Would you like to look for something a little bit more expensive?

¿Desea buscar algo un poco más caro?
[day-**SAY**-ah/ boos-**CAR**/ **AHL**-goh/ oon/ **POH**-koh/ **MAHS**/ **KAH**-roh⚥]

5. I will keep looking.

Voy a seguir buscando.
[**VOY**/ ah/ say-**GEAR**/ boos-**KAHN**-doh]

6. I will let you know if I find something.

Le avisaré si encuentro algo.
[lay/ ah-vee-sah-**RAY**/ see/ enn-**KWEN**-troh/ **AHL**-goh]

Unit B: Reviewing Possible Properties
CD One, Track 17

1. I have good news.

Le tengo buenas noticias.
[lay/ **TEN**-goh/ **BWAY**-nahs/ noh-**TEE**-see+ahs]

2. We have:

Tenemos:
[tay-**NAY**-mohs]

- some properties you might like.

  • algunas propiedades que le pueden interesar.
  [ahl-**GOO**-nahs/ proh-pee+ay-**DAH**-days/ kay/ lay/ **PWAY**-den/ een-tay-ray-**SAR**]

- pictures.

  • fotos.
  [**FOH**-tohs]

- the addresses.

  • las direcciones.
  [lahs/ dee-reck-**SEE+OH**-nays]

- the keys.

  • las llaves.
  [lahs/ **YAH**-vays]

3. Please come to my office.

Por favor, venga a mi oficina.
[por/ fah-**VOHR**/ **VENN**-gah/ ah/ mee/ oh-fee-**SEE**-nah]

Chapter 8:
Follow-up Interview After Prequalification (cont.)

English	Spanish Version & [Phonetic Encoding]

Unit B: Reviewing Possible Properties (cont.)

4. This is what I found. (point to print out or picture)

Esto es lo que encontré.
[**ESS**-toh/ **ESS**/ loh/ kay/ enn-cone-**TRAY**]

5. Point to the one you like the most.

Señale la que más le gusta.
[say-**NYAH**-lay/ lah/ kay/ **MAHS**/ lay/ **GOOSE**-tah]

Unit C: Reviewing Buyer-Found Properties
CD One, Track 18

1. Show me what you have found. (if customer looked at magazine or website)

Muéstreme lo que encontró.
[**MWAYS**-tray-may/ loh/ kay/ enn-cone-**TROH**]

2. Did you find it:

¿La encontró:
[lah/ enn-cone-**TROH**]

   • on the internet?

   • en el internet?
   [enn/ ell/ een-tair-**NET**☝]

   • through a realtor sign?

   • por un letrero de bienes raíces?
   [por/ oon/ lay-**TRAY**-roh/ day/ **BEE+AY**-nays/ rrah-**EE**-says☝]

   • in a newspaper?

   • en un periódico?
   [enn/ oon/ pay-**REE+OH**-dee-koh☝]

   • in a realty magazine?

   • en una revista de propiedades?
   [enn/ **OO**-nah/ ray-**VEES**-tah/ day/ proh-pee+ay-**DAH**-days☝]

   • in a realtor brochure?

   • en un folleto de bienes raíces?
   [enn/ oon/ foh-**YAY**-toh/ day/ **BEE+AY**-nays/ rrah-**EE**-says☝]

3. Which one?

¿En cuál?
[enn/ **KWAHL**☝]

4. What number is it?*

¿Qué número es?
[**KAY**/ **NOO**-may-roh/ **ESS**☝]

5. Let's try to get an appointment to see it.

Tratemos de hacer una cita para verla.
[trah-**TAY**-mohs/ day/ ah-**SAIR**/ **OO**-nah/ **SEE**-tah/ **PAH**-rah/ **VAIR**-lah]

---

* *See Chapter 4, "Numbers" on page 7.*

Chapter 9:
Property Descriptions

English	Spanish Version & [Phonetic Encoding]

CD Two, Track 03

1. Let me tell you about this property.

Permítame darle información acerca de esta propiedad.
[pair-**MEE**-tah-may/ **DAR**-lay/ een-for-mah-**SEE+OHN**/ day/**ESS**-tah/ proh-pee+ay-**DAHD**]

2. It's on (*street/ avenue/ highway/ road's name*).

Está en (*street/ avenue/ highway/ road's name*).
[ess-**TAH**/ enn/ ___]

3. It's at (*neighborhood/ address*).

Está en (*neighborhood/ address*).
[ess-**TAH**/ enn/ ___]

4. The lot area is (#) by (#) feet.

El área de la propiedad es de (#) por (#) pies.*
[ell/ **AH**-ray-ah/ day/ lah/ proh-pee+ay-**DAHD**/ **ESS**/ day/ ___/ por/ ___/ **PEE+ACE**]

5. The heated and cooled area is (#) square feet.

El área con calefacción y aire acondicionado es de (#) pies cuadrados.
[ell/ **AH**-ray-ah/ cone/ kah-lay-fax-**SEE+OHN**/ ee/ **EYE**-ray/ ah-cone-dee-see+oh-**NAH**-doh/ **ESS**/ day/ ___/ **PEE+ACE**/ kwah-**DRAH**-dohs]

6. It's near:

Está cerca de:
[ess-**TAH**/ **SAIR**-kah/ day]

   • (*name or number*) street.

   • la calle (*name or number*).
     [lah/ **KAH**-yay/ ___]

   • (*name or #*) avenue.

   • la avenida (*name or #*).
     [lah/ ah-vay-**NEE**-dah/ ___]

   • (*name or #*) highway.

   • la carretera (*name or #*).
     [lah/ kah-rray-**TAY**-rah/ ___]

   • (*name*) school.

   • la escuela (*name*).
     [lah/ ess-**KWAY**-lah/ ___]

   • (*name*) supermarket.

   • el supermercado (*name*).
     ell/ soo-pair-mair-**KAH**-doh/ ___]

   • (*name*) mall.

   • el centro comercial (*name*).
     [ell/ **SEN**-troh/ koh-mair-**SEE+AHL**/ ___]

7. There is a security guard.

Hay vigilancia.
[**EYE**/ vee-hee-**LAHN**-see+ah]

8. There is an alarm system.

Hay un sistema de alarma.
[**EYE**/ oon/ sees-**TAY**-mah/ day/ ah-**LAHR**-mah]

---

* *See Chapter 4, "Numbers" on page 7.*

Chapter 9:
Property Descriptions (cont.)

English	Spanish Version & [Phonetic Encoding]
9. The entrance is monitored.	La entrada está vigilada. [lah/ enn-**TRAH**-dah/ ess-**TAH**/ vee-hee-**LAH**-dah]
10. You need a code to enter.	Necesita un código para entrar. [nay-say-**SEE**-tah/ oon/ **KOH**-dee-goh/ **PAH**-rah/ enn-**TRAHR**]
11. It has:*	Tiene: [**TEE+AY**-nay]

OR

It doesn't have:	**OR** No tiene: [**NOH**/ **TEE+AY**-nay]
• one story.	• un piso. [oon/ **PEE**-soh]
• (#) stories.	• (#) pisos.† [___/ **PEE**-sohs]
• one bedroom.	• una recámara.‡ [**OO**-nah/ rray-**KAH**-mah-rah]
• (#) bedrooms.	• (#) recámaras. [___/ rray-**KAH**-mah-rahs]
• one bathroom.	• un baño. [oon/ **BAH**-nyoh]
• one and a half bathrooms.	• un baño y medio. [oon/ **BAH**-nyoh/ ee/ **MAY**-dee+oh]
• (#) bathrooms.	• (#) baños. [___/ **BAH**-nyohs]
• (#) and a half bathrooms.	• (#) baños y medio. [___/ **BAH**-nyohs/ ee/ **MAY**-dee+oh]
• a one-car garage.	• un garaje para un auto. [oon/ gah-**RAH**-hay/ **PAH**-rah/ oon/ **OW**-toh]
• a two-car garage.	• un garaje para dos autos. [oon/ gah-**RAH**-hay/ **PAH**-rah/ **DOHS**/ **OW**-tohs]
• a three-car garage.	• un garaje para tres autos. [oon/ gah-**RAH**-hay/ **PAH**-rah/ **TRACE**/ **OW**-tohs]
• a carport.	• una cochera. [**OO**-nah/ koh-**CHAY**-rah]
• a bonus room.	• un cuarto extra. [oon/ **KWAHR**-toh/ **EX**-trah]
• a (formal) dining room.	• un comedor (formal). [oon/ koh-may-**DOHR**/ (for-**MAHL**)]

---

* See "Appendix H: Property Features Checklist" on page 73.
† See Chapter 4, "Numbers" on page 7.
‡ See "Appendix A: Cultural Notes" on page 63.

Chapter 9:
Property Descriptions (cont.)

English	Spanish Version & [Phonetic Encoding]
11. It has: (cont.)	Tiene: [**TEE+AY**-nay]
OR	*OR*
It doesn't have: (cont.)	No tiene: [**NOH**/ **TEE+AY**-nay]
• a living room.	• una sala. [**OO**-nah/ **SAH**-lah]
• a family room *OR* a den.	• una sala de estar. [**OO**-nah/ **SAH**-lah/ day/ ess-**TAR**]
• a game room.	• un cuarto de juegos. [oon/ **KWAR**-toh/ day/ **HOO+AY**-gohs]
• an inside laundry room.	• un cuarto de lavado dentro de la casa. [oon/ **KWAHR**-toh/ day/ lah-**VAH**-doh/ **DEN**-troh/ day/ lah/ **KAH**-sah]
• an outside laundry room.	• un cuarto de lavado fuera de la casa. [oon/ **KWAHR**-toh/ day/ lah-**VAH**-doh/ **FWAY**-rah/ day/ lah/ **KAH**-sah]
• a wood burning fireplace.	• una chimenea. [**OO**-nah/ chee-may-**NAY**-ah]
• a gas burning fireplace.	• una chimenea de gas. [**OO**-nah/ chee-may-**NAY**-ah/ day/ **GAHS**]
• central air conditioning.	• aire acondicionado central. [**EYE**-ray/ ah-cone-dee-see+oh-**NAH**-doh/ sen-**TRAHL**]
• *(#)* central air conditioning units.*	• *(#)* unidades de aire acondicionado. [___/ oo-nee-**DAH**-days/ day/ **EYE**-ray/ ah-cone-dee-see+oh-**NAH**-doh]
• gas air conditioning.	• aire acondicionado de gas. [**EYE**-ray/ ah-cone-dee-see+oh-**NAH**-doh/ day/ **GAHS**]
• electric air conditioning.	• aire acondicionado eléctrico. [**EYE**-ray/ ah-cone-dee-see+oh-**NAH**-doh/ ay-**LECK**-tree-koh]
• window units.	• unidades de aire acondicionado en las ventanas. [oo-nee-**DAH**-days/ day/ **EYE**-ray/ ah-cone-dee-see+oh-**NAH**-doh/ enn/ lahs/ venn-**TAH**-nahs]
• ceiling fans.	• abanicos de techo. [ah-bah-**NEE**-kohs/ day/ **TAY**-choh]

See Chapter 4, "Numbers" on page 7.

Chapter 9:
Property Descriptions (cont.)

English	Spanish Version & [Phonetic Encoding]
11. It has: (cont.)	Tiene: [**TEE+AY**-nay]
OR	**OR**
It doesn't have: (cont.)	No tiene: [**NOH**/ **TEE+AY**-nay]
• central (gas) heating.	• calefacción central (de gas). [kah-lay-fax-**SEE+OHN**/ sen-**TRAHL**/ (day/ **GAHS**)]
• gas heating.	• calefacción de gas. [kah-lay-fax-**SEE+OHN**/ day/ **GAHS**]
• electric heating.	• calefacción eléctrica. [kah-lay-fax-**SEE+OHN**/ ay-**LECK**-tree-kah]
• a gas water heater.	• un calentador de agua de gas. [oon/ kah-len-tah-**DOHR**/ day/ **AH**-gwah/ day/ **GAHS**]
• an electric water heater.	• un calentador de agua eléctrico. [oon/ kah-len-tah-**DOHR**/ day/ **AH**-gwah/ ay-**LECK**-tree-koh]
• (#) water heaters.	• (#) calentadores de agua.* [__/ kah-len-tah-**DOH**-rays/ day/ **AH**-gwah]
• a big kitchen.	• una cocina grande. [**OO**-nah/ koh-**SEE**-nah/ **GRAHN**-day]
• (new) appliances.	• electrodomésticos (nuevos). [ay-leck-troh-doh-**MAYS**-tee-kohs/ (**NWAY**-vohs)]
• a basement.	• un sótano. [oon/ **SOH**-tah-noh]
• an attic.	• un ático. [oon/ **AH**-tee-koh]
• a balcony.	• un balcón. [oon/ bahl-**CONE**]
• an office.	• una oficina. [**OO**-nah/ oh-fee-**SEE**-nah]
• an alarm system.	• un sistema de alarma. [oon/ sees-**TAY**-mah/ day/ ah-**LAHR**-mah]
• a front porch.	• un pórtico frontal. [oon/ **POR**-tee-koh/ frohn-**TAHL**]
• a sun porch.	• un pórtico que da al sol. [oon/ **POR**-tee-koh/ kay/ **DAH**/ ahl/ **SOHL**]
• a screen porch.	• un pórtico rodeado de tela metálica. [oon/ **POR**-tee-koh/ rroh-day-**AH**-doh/ day/ **TAY**-lah/ may-**TAH**-lee-kah]
• a skylight.	• un tragaluz. [oon/ trah-gah-**LOOSE**]

---

* See Chapter 4, "Numbers" on page 7.

©2005, Command Spanish®, Inc. – Consumer Division

Chapter 9:
Property Descriptions (cont.)

English	Spanish Version & [Phonetic Encoding]
11. It has: (cont.)	Tiene: [**TEE+AY**-nay]
OR	**OR**
It doesn't have: (cont.)	No tiene: [**NOH**/ **TEE+AY**-nay]
• a (covered) deck.	• una terraza (cubierta). [**OO**-nah/ tay-**RRAH**-sah/ (koo-**BEE+AIR**-tah)]
• a sunroom.	• un "sunroom". [oon/ *SUNROOM*]
• a tool room.	• un cuarto de herramientas. [oon/ **KWAHR**-toh/ day/ ay-rrah-**MEE+ENN**-tahs]
• stairs.	• escaleras. [ess-kah-**LAY**-rahs]
• drapes.	• cortinas. [core-**TEE**-nahs]
• wood blinds.	• persianas de madera. [pair-**SEE+AH**-nahs/ day/ mah-**DAY**-rah]
• Venetian blinds.	• persianas. [pair-**SEE+AH**-nahs]
• vinyl windows.	• ventanas de vinil. [venn-**TAH**-nahs/ day/ vee-**NEEL**]
• (good) insulation.	• (buen) aislamiento. [(**BWAIN**)/ ah-ees-lah-**MEE+ENN**-toh]
• built-in shelves.	• repisas empotradas. [rray-**PEE**-sahs/ emm-poh-**TRAH**-dahs]
• carpet.	• alfombra. [ahl-**FOAM**-brah]
• hardwood flooring.	• pisos de madera. [**PEE**-sohs/ day/ mah-**DAY**-rah]
• parquet flooring.	• pisos de parquet. [**PEE**-sohs/ day/ par-**KAY**]
• linoleum flooring.	• pisos de linóleo. [**PEE**-sohs/ day/ lee-**NOH**-lay-oh]
• tile flooring.	• baldosas. [bahl-**DOH**-sahs]
• cathedral ceiling.	• techo estilo catedral. [**TAY**-choh/ ess-**TEE**-loh/ kah-tay-**DRAHL**]
• a pool.	• una alberca.* [**OO**-nah/ ahl-**BAIR**-kah]
• insulated windows.	• ventanas con aislamiento. [venn-**TAH**-nahs/ cone/ ah-ees-lah-**MEE+ENN**-toh]

* *See "Appendix A: Culutral Notes" on page 63.*

Chapter 9:
Property Descriptions (cont.)

English	Spanish Version & [Phonetic Encoding]

11. It has: (cont.)

OR

It doesn't have: (cont.)

- double hung windows.

- single hung windows.

- aluminum windows.

- a yard.

- a shop (wired with electricity).

- trees.

- a lawn.

- shrubs.

- shingles.

- a metal roof.

- a tile roof.

- a septic tank.

- a treatment plant.

- a bar.

- a bar-b-que pit.

12. The outside is:

- (painted) wood.

- brick.

Tiene:
[**TEE+AY**-nay]

OR

No tiene:
[**NOH**/ **TEE+AY**-nay]

- ventanas de guillotina doble.
  [venn-**TAH**-nahs/ **DOH**-blay]

- ventanas de guillotina sencilla.
  [venn-**TAH**-nahs/ sen-**SEE**-yah]

- ventanas de aluminio.
  [venn-**TAH**-nahs/ day/ ah-loo-**MEE**-nee+oh]

- un jardín.
  [oon/ har-**DEEN**]

- un taller (con electricidad).
  [oon/ tah-**YAIR**/ (cone/ ay-leck-tree-see-**DAHD**)]

- árboles.
  [**ARE**-boh-lays]

- pasto.*
  [**PAHS**-toh]

- arbustos.
  [are-**BOOS**-tohs]

- tejamanil de asfalto.
  [tay-hah-mah-**NEEL**/ day/ ahs-**FAHL**-toh]

- techo de metal.
  [**TAY**-choh/ day/ may-**TAHL**]

- techo de teja.
  [**TAY**-choh/ day/ **TAY**-hah]

- un tanque séptico.
  [oon/ **TAHN**-kay/ **SEP**-tee-koh]

- una planta de tratamiento de aguas negras.
  [**OO**-nah/ **PLAHN**-tah/ day/ trah-tah-**MEE+ENN**-toh/ day/ **AH**-gwahs/ **NAY**-grahs]

- un bar.
  [oon/ **BAR**]

- un asador empotrado.
  [oon/ ah-sah-**DOHR**/ emm-poh-**TRAH**-doh]

El exterior es de:
[ell/ ex-tay-ree-**OR**/ **ESS**/ day]

- madera (pintada).
  [mah-**DAY**-rah/ (peen-**TAH**-dah)]

- ladrillo.
  [lah-**DREE**-yoh]

---

* *See "Appendix A: Culural Notes" on page 63.*

Chapter 9:
Property Descriptions (cont.)

English	Spanish Version & [Phonetic Encoding]
12. The outside is: (cont.)	El exterior es de: [ell/ ex-tay-ree-**OR**/ **ESS**/ day]
• vinyl siding.	• vinil. [vee-**NEEL**]
• aluminum siding.	• aluminio. [ah-loo-**MEE**-nee+oh]
13. The bedroom has:	La recámara tiene: [lah/ rray-**KAH**-mah-rah/ **TEE+AY**-nay]
OR The bedroom doesn't have:	*OR* La recámara no tiene: [lah/ rray-**KAH**-mah-rah/ **NOH**/ **TEE+AY**-nay]
• a walk-in closet.	• un vestidor. [oon/ vays-tee-**DOHR**]
• two separate closets.	• dos closets separados. [**DOHS**/ *CLOSETS*/ say-pah-**RAH**-dohs]
• a bathroom.	• un baño. [oon/ **BAH**-nyoh]
14. The bathroom has:	El baño tiene: [ell/ **BAH**-nyoh/ **TEE+AY**-nay]
OR The bathroom doesn't have:	*OR* El baño no tiene: [ell/ **BAH**-nyoh/ **NOH**/ **TEE+AY**-nay]
• a (separate) shower stall.	• una regadera (separada).* [**OO**-nah/ rray-gah-**DAY**-rah/ (say-pah-**RAH**-dah)]
• a bathtub.	• una tina. [**OO**-nah/ **TEE**-nah]
• a whirlpool tub.	• una tina de masajes con chorro de agua y burbujas. [**OO**-nah/ **TEE**-nah/ day/ mah-**SAH**-hays/ cone/ **CHOH**-rroh/ day/ **AH**-gwah/ ee/ boor-**BOO**-hahs]
• a jacuzzi.	• un jacuzzi. [oon/ *JACUZZI*]
• two separate sinks.	• dos lavamanos separados.† [**DOHS**/ lah-vah-**MAH**-nohs/ say-pah-**RAH**-dohs]
• a window.	• una ventana. [**OO**-nah/ ven-**TAH**-nah]
• an exhaust fan.	• un extractor de olores. [oon/ ex-trahk-**TORE**/ day/ oh-**LOH**-rays]
• cabinets.	• gabinetes. [gah-bee-**NAY**-tays]

---

* *See "Appendix A: Cultural Notes" on page 63.*
† *See "Appendix A: Cultural Notes" on page 63.*

Chapter 9:
Property Descriptions (cont.)

English	Spanish Version & [Phonetic Encoding]

14. The bathroom has: (cont.)
El baño tiene:
[ell/ **BAH**-nyoh/ **TEE+AY**-nay]

OR

The bathroom doesn't have: (cont.)
El baño no tiene:
[ell/ **BAH**-nyoh/ **NOH**/ **TEE+AY**-nay]

- a linen closet.
un closet para la ropa de cama.
[oon/ *CLOSET*/ **PAH**-rah/ lah/ **RROH**-pah/ day/ **KAH**-mah]

- a walk-in closet.
un vestidor.
[oon/ vays-tee-**DOHR**]

- access to *(part of the home)*.
acceso a *(part of the home)*.
[ax-**SAY**-soh/ ah/ ___]

15. It's made of:
Está hecho de:
[ess-**TAH**/ **AY**-choh/ day]

- ceramic.
cerámica.
[say-**RAH**-mee-kah]

- porcelain.
porcelana.
[por-say-**LAH**-nah]

- fiberglass.
fibra de vidrio.
[**FEE**-brah/ day/ **VEE**-dree+oh]

- plastic.
plástico.
[**PLAHS**-tee-koh]

16. The garage has:
El garaje tiene:
[ell/ gah-**RAH**-hay/ **TEE+AY**-nay]

OR

The garage doesn't have:
El garaje no tiene:
[ell/ gah-**RAH**-hay/ **NOH**/ **TEE+AY**-nay]

- an electric door.
puerta eléctrica.
[**PWAIR**-tah/ ay-**LECK**-tree-kah]

- shelves.
repisas.
[rray-**PEE**-sahs]

- storage space.
espacio para guardar cosas.
[ess-**PAH**-see+oh/ **PAH**-rah/ goo+are-**DAHR**/ **KOH**-sahs]

- access to the house.
acceso a la casa.
[ax-**SAY**-soh/ ah/ lah/ **KAH**-sah]

- access to the attic.
acceso al ático.
[ax-**SAY**-soh/ ahl/ **AH**-tee-koh]

Chapter 9:
Property Descriptions (cont.)

English	Spanish Version & [Phonetic Encoding]
17. The laundry room has:	El cuarto de lavado tiene: [ell/ **KWAHR**-toh/ day/ lah-**VAH**-doh/ **TEE+AY**-nay]
<u>OR</u>	<u>OR</u>
The laundry room doesn't have:	El cuarto de lavado no tiene: [ell/ **KWAHR**-toh/ day/ lah-**VAH**-doh/ **NOH**/ **TEE+AY**-nay]
• a washer.	• una lavadora. [**OO**-nah/ lah-vah-**DOH**-rah]
• a dryer.	• una secadora. [**OO**-nah/ say-kah-**DOH**-rah]
• air conditioner.	• aire acondicionado. [**EYE**-ray/ ah-cone-dee-see+oh-**NAH**-doh]
• cabinets.	• gabinetes. [gah-bee-**NAY**-tays]
• freezer space.	• espacio para un congelador. [ess-**PAH**-see+oh/ **PAH**-rah/ oon/ cone-hay-lah-**DOHR**]
18. The kitchen has:	La cocina tiene: [lah/ koh-**SEE**-nah/ **TEE+AY**-nay]
<u>OR</u>	<u>OR</u>
The kitchen doesn't have:	La cocina no tiene: [lah/ koh-**SEE**-nah/ noh/ **TEE+AY**-nay]
• a stove.	• una estufa. [**OO**-nah/ ess-**TOO**-fah]
• a stove top.	• una estufa sin horno. [**OO**-nah/ ess-**TOO**-fah/ seen/ **OR**-noh]
• a gas range.	• una estufa de gas. [**OO**-nah/ ess-**TOO**-fah/ day/ **GAHS**]
• an electric range.	• una estufa eléctrica. [**OO**-nah/ ess-**TOO**-fah/ ay-**LECK**-tree-kah]
• a built-in oven.	• un horno empotrado. [oon/ **OR**-noh/ emm-poh-**TRAH**-doh]
• a separate oven.	• un horno separado. [oon/ **OR**-noh/ say-pah-**RAH**-doh]
• a gas oven.	• un horno de gas. [oon/ **OR**-noh/ day/ **GAHS**]
• an electric oven.	• un horno eléctrico. [oon/ **OR**-noh/ ay-**LECK**-tree-koh]
• a microwave oven.	• un horno de microondas. [oon/ **OR**-noh/ day/ mee-kroh-**OHN**-dahs]
• an over the range microwave.	• un horno de microondas sobre la estufa. [oon/ **OR**-noh/ day/ mee-kroh-**OHN**-dahs/ **SOH**-bray/ lah/ ess-**TOO**-fah]

Chapter 9:
Property Descriptions (cont.)

English	Spanish Version & [Phonetic Encoding]
18. The kitchen has: (cont.)	La cocina tiene: [lah/ koh-**SEE**-nah/ **TEE+AY**-nay]
OR	**OR**
The kitchen doesn't have: (cont.)	La cocina no tiene: [lah/ koh-**SEE**-nah/ noh/ **TEE+AY**-nay]
• a built-in microwave.	• un horno de microondas empotrado. [oon/ **OR**-noh/ day/ mee-kroh-**OHN**-dahs/ emm-poh-**TRAH**-doh]
• a dishwasher.	• una lavaplatos. [**OO**-nah/ lah-vah-**PLAH**-tohs]
• a refrigerator with freezer.	• un refrigerador con congelador. [oon/ rray-free-hay-rah-**DOHR**/ cone/ cone-hay-lah-**DOHR**]
• a separate freezer.	• un congelador separado. [oon/ cone-hay-lah-**DOHR**/ say-pah-**RAH**-doh]
• a double kitchen sink.	• un fregadero doble.* [oon/ fray-gah-**DAY**-roh/ **DOH**-blay]
• Formica countertops.	• superficie de Formica. [soo-pair-**FEE**-see+ay/ day/ FORMICA]
• tile countertops.	• superficie de baldosa. [soo-pair-**FEE**-see+ay/ day/ bahl-**DOH**-sah]
• marble countertops.	• superficie de mármol. [soo-pair-**FEE**-see+ay/ day/ **MAHR**-mohl]
• ceramic countertops.	• superficie de cerámica. [soo-pair-**FEE**-see+ay/ day/ say-**RAH**-mee-kah]
• granite countertops.	• superficie de granito. [soo-pair-**FEE**-see+ay/ day/ grah-**NEE**-toh]
• a dining area.	• un área para comer. [oon/ **AH**-ray-ah/ **PAH**-rah/ koh-**MAIR**]
• a work island.	• una "isla" para trabajar en la cocina. [**OO**-nah/ **EES**-lah/ **PAH**-rah/ trah-bah-**HAHR**/ enn/ lah/ koh-**SEE**-nah]
• a cabinet pantry.	• una alacena. [**OO**-nah/ ah-lah-**SAY**-nah]
• a trash compactor.	• un compactador de basura. [oon/ comb-pack-tah-**DOHR**/ day/ bah-**SOO**-rah]
• a garbage disposal.	• un triturador de basura. [oon/ tree-too-rah-**DOHR**/ day/ bah-**SOO**-rah]
• an ice maker.	• una máquina para hacer hielo. [**OO**-nah/ **MAH**-kee-nah/ **PAH**-rah/ ah-**SAIR**/ **YAY**-loh]

---
* *See "Appendix A: Cultural Notes" on page 63.*

Chapter 9:
Property Descriptions (cont.)

English	Spanish Version & [Phonetic Encoding]
19. According to the owner:	Según el dueño: [say-**GOON**/ ell/ **DWAY**-nyoh]
• the property taxes are *(amount)*.	• los impuestos son *(#)* dólares.* [lohs/ eem-**PWAYS**-tohs/ **SOHN**/ ___/ **DOH**-lay-rays]
• the utility costs average *(amount)*.	• el costo promedio de los servicios es de *(#)* dólares. [ell/ **KOHS**-toh/ proh-**MAY**-dee+oh/ day/ lohs/ sair-**VEE**-see+ohs/ **ESS**/ day/ ___/ **DOH**-lah-rays]
• this property is in *(name)* school district.	• esta propiedad está en el distrito escolar *(name)*. [**ESS**-tah/ proh-pee+ay-**DAHD**/ ess-**TAH**/ enn/ ell/ dees-**TREE**-toh/ ess-koh-**LAHR**/ ___]
20. *(Amount)* is the average monthly bill for:	*(#)* dólares es el promedio mensual de la cuenta de: [___/ **DOH**-lah-rays/ **ESS**/ ell/ proh-**MAY**-dee+oh/ men-**SOO+AHL**/ day/ lah/ **KWEN**-tah/ day]
• electricity.	• la luz. [lah/ **LOOSE**]
• gas.	• el gas. [ell/ **GAHS**]
• water.	• el agua. [ell/ **AH**-gwah]
• sewage.	• el alcantarillado. [ell/ ahl-kahn-tah-ree-**YAH**-doh]
• garbage.	• la basura. [lah/ bah-**SOO**-rah]

---

* See Chapter 4, "Numbers" on page 7 and "Appendix E: Money Issues" on page 66.

Chapter 10:
Preparing for the Property Visits

English	Spanish Version & [Phonetic Encoding]

CD Two, Track 04

1. I've arranged for us to see (#) properties.

Hice citas para que veamos (#) propiedades.*
[**EE**-say/ **SEE**-tahs/ **PAH**-rah/ kay/ vay-**AH**-mohs/ ___/ proh-pee+ay-**DAH**-days]

2. Would you like to:

¿Desea:
[day-**SAY**-ah]

   • go and look at it?

   • ir a verla?
[**EAR**/ ah/ **VAIR**-lah ♀]

   • go and look at it from the outside?

   • ir a verla por fuera?
[**EAR**/ ah/ **VAIR**-lah/ por/ **FWAY**-rah ♀]

   • go with me?

   • ir conmigo?
[**EAR**/ cone-**MEE**-goh ♀]

   • go in my car?

   • ir en mi auto?
[**EAR**/ enn/ mee/ **OW**-toh ♀]

   • go in your car?

   • ir en su auto?
[**EAR**/ enn/ soo/ **OW**-toh ♀]

   • go on your own and let me know if you like it?

   • ir por su cuenta y decirme si le gusta?
[**EAR**/ por/ soo/ **KWENN**-tah/ ee/ day-**SEER**-may/ see/ lay/ **GOOSE**-tah ♀]

   • go now?

   • ir ahora?
[**EAR**/ ah-**OH**-rah ♀]

   • go another day?

   • ir otro día?
[**EAR**/ **OH**-troh/ **DEE**-ah ♀]

   • go another time?

   • ir a otra hora?
[**EAR**/ ah/ **OH**-trah/ **OH**-rah ♀]

3. Point to the most convenient day. (show calendar)

Señale el día más conveniente.
[say-**NYAH**-lay/ ell/ **DEE**-ah **MAHS**/ cone-vay-**NEE+ENN**-tay]

4. Point to the most convenient time. (show daily planner)

Señale la hora más conveniente.
[say-**NYAH**-lay/ lah/ **OH**-rah/ **MAHS**/ cone-vay-**NEE+ENN**-tay]

5. I can go.

Puedo ir.
[**PWAY**-doh/ **EAR**]

OR

OR

I cannot go.

No puedo ir.
[**NOH**/ **PWAY**-doh/ **EAR**]

6. Let's go.

Vamos.
[**VAH**-mohs]

See Chapter 4, "Numbers" on page 7.

Chapter 10:
Preparing for the Property Visits (cont.)

English	Spanish Version & [Phonetic Encoding]
7. We can meet:	Podemos reunirnos: [poh-**DAY**-mohs/ ray+oo-**NEAR**-nohs]
• here.	• aquí. [ah-**KEY**]
• there.	• allá. [ah-**YAH**]
• at my office.	• en mi oficina. [enn/ mee/ oh-fee-**SEE**-nah]
• at your house.	• en su casa. [enn/ soo/ **KAH**-sah]
• at (*name of place*).	• en (*name of place*). [enn/ ___]
• on (*day of the week*).*	• el (*day of the week*). [ell/ ___]
• at (*time*).†	• a la(s) (*time*). [ah/ lah(s)/ ___]
8. Do you know where that is?	¿Sabe dónde queda? [**SAH**-bay/ **DOAN**-day/ **KAY**-dah⇗]
9. Let's look at this map. (point to map)	Veamos este mapa. [vay-**AH**-mohs/ **ESS**-tay/ **MAH**-pah]
10. We are here. (point)	Estamos aquí. [ess-**TAH**-mohs/ ah-**KEY**]
11. It's here. (point)	Queda aquí. [**KAY**-dah/ ah-**KEY**]
12. Go this way. (show route on map)‡	Vaya por aquí. [**VAH**-yah/ por/ ah-**KEY**]
13. If you have to cancel our appointment, please call me at (#).	Si tiene que cancelar la cita, por favor, llámeme al (#).§ [see/ **TEE+AY**-nay/ kay/ kahn-say-**LAHR**/ lah/ **SEE**-tah/ por/ fah-**VOHR**/ **YAH**-may-may/ ahl/ ___]

* See "Appendix F: Announcing Dates and Times" on page 67.
† See "Appendix F: Announcing Dates and Times" on page 67.
‡ See "Appendix G: Giving Directions" on page 69.
§ See Chapter 4, "Numbers" on page 7.

Chapter 11:
At an Open House

English	Spanish Version & [Phonetic Encoding]

CD Two, Track 05

1. Welcome.
   Bienvenido.
   [bee+enn-vay-**NEE**-doh]

2. Please look around.
   Por favor, entre y mire.
   [por/ fah-**VOHR**/ **ENN**-tray/ ee/ **MEE**-ray]

3. Would you like some? (point to refreshments)
   ¿Desea?
   [day-**SAY**-ah ⇧]

4. Help yourself.
   Por favor, sírvase.
   [por/ fah-**VOHR**/ **SEER**-vah-say]

5. Let me know if you have any questions.
   Dígame si tiene preguntas.
   [**DEE**-gah-may/ see/ **TEE+AY**-nay/ pray-**GOON**-tahs]

6. Please sign in.
   Por favor, escriba su nombre aquí.
   [por/ fah-**VOHR**/ ess-**KREE**-bah/ soo/ **NOME**-bray/ ah-**KEE**]

7. May I call you?
   ¿Puedo llamarle?
   [**PWAY**-doh/ yah-**MAR**-lay ⇧]

8. Here's my card. (hand out business card)
   Esta es mi tarjeta.
   [**ESS**-tah/ **ESS**/ mee/ tar-**HAY**-tah]

9. Here is information about this property. (hand out info sheet)
   Esta es información acerca de esta propiedad.
   [**ESS**-tah/ **ESS**/ een-for-mah-**SEE+OHN**/ ah-**SAIR**-kah/ day/ **ESS**-tah/ proh-pee+ay-**DAHD**]

Chapter 12:
Sales Talk

English	Spanish Version & [Phonetic Encoding]

CD Two, Track 06

1. This property is not likely to lose its value.

Esta propiedad no tiende a devaluarse.
[**ESS**-tah/ proh-pee+ay-**DAHD**/ **NOH**/ **TEE+ENN**-day/ ah/ day-vah-**LOO+ARE**-say]

2. Property values are:

El valor de la propiedad está:
[ell/ vah-**LOHR**/ day/ lah/ proh-pee+ay-**DAHD**/ ess-**TAH**]

   • depreciating.

   • bajando.
      [bah-**HAHN**-doh]

   • stable.

   • estable.
      [ess-**TAH**-blay]

   • appreciating.

   • subiendo.
      [soo-**BEE+ENN**-doh]

3. This is a:

Este es un:
[**ESS**-tay/ **ESS**/ oon]

   • great place to raise the family.

   • buen lugar para una familia.
      [**BWAIN**/ loo-**GAR**/ **PAH**-rah/ **OO**-nah/ fah-**MEE**-lee+ah]

   • nice neighborhood.

   • buen vecindario.*
      [**BWAIN**/ vay-seen-**DAH**-ree+oh]

   • safe neighborhood.

   • vecindario seguro.
      [vay-seen-**DAH**-ree+oh/ say-**GOO**-roh]

4. The neighborhood features:

El barrio se destaca por:
[ell/ **BAH**-rree+oh/ say/ days-**TAH**-kah/ por]

   • a good school system.

   • estar en un buen sistema escolar.
      [ess-**TAR**/ enn/ oon/ **BWAIN**/ sees-**TAY**-mah/ ess-koh-**LAHR**]

   • a playground.

   • tener un parque.
      [tay-**NAIR**/ oon/ **PAR**-kay]

   • a community pool.

   • tener una alberca comunitaria.
      [tay-**NAIR**/ **OO**-nah/ ahl-**BAIR**-kah/ koh-moo-nee-**TAH**-ree+ah]

   • a lake.

   • tener un lago.
      [tay-**NAIR**/ oon/ **LAH**-goh]

5. This is just what you are looking for.

Esta es justo lo que usted busca.
[**ESS**-tah/ **ESS**/ **HOOS**-toh/ loh/ kay/ oose-**TED**/ **BOOS**-kah]

---

* *See "Appendix A: Cultural Notes" on page 63.*

Chapter 12:
Sales Talk (cont.)

English	Spanish Version & [Phonetic Encoding]
6. Is this:	¿Es esto: [**ESS**/ **ESS**-toh]
• what you need?	lo que necesita? [loh/ kay/ nay-say-**SEE**-tah♀]
• what you are looking for?	lo que busca? [loh/ kay/ **BOOS**-kah♀]
• what you had in mind?	lo que se imaginaba? [loh/ kay/ say/ ee-mah-hee-**NAH**-bah♀]
7. What's missing?	¿Qué le falta? [**KAY**/ lay/ **FAHL**-tah♀]
8. It has good access to:	Tiene buen acceso a: [**TEE+AY**-nay/ **BWAIN**/ ax-**SAY**-soh/ ah]
• highway *(name)*.	• la carretera *(name)*. [lah/ kah-rray-**TAY**-rah/ ___]
• the *(name)* mall.	• el centro comercial *(name)*. [ell/ **SEN**-troh/ koh-mair-**SEE+AHL**/ ___]
• *(name)* school.	• la escuela *(name)*. [lah/ ess-**KWAY**-lah/ ___]

Chapter 13:
Visiting Properties

English	Spanish Version & [Phonetic Encoding]

CD Two, Track 07

1. Let's go through here. (point)

   Vayamos por aquí.
   [vah-**YAH**-mohs/ por/ ah-**KEY**]

2. Follow me.

   Sígame.
   [**SEE**-gah-may]

3. This way. (show)

   Por aquí.
   [por/ ah-**KEY**]

4. Come in.

   Pase.
   [**PAH**-say]

5. The property line goes from about here to there. (point)

   El lindero va de aquí a allá.
   [ell/ leen-**DAY**-roh/ **VAH**/ day/ ah-**KEY**/ ah/ ah-**YAH**]

6. The easement goes through here. (point)

   La zona de servidumbre va por aquí.
   [lah/ **SOH**-nah/ day/ sair-vee-**DOOM**-bray/ **VAH**/ por/ ah-**KEY**]

7. This is: (point)

   OR

   This is not: (point)

   Esto es:
   [**ESS**-toh/ **ESS**]

   OR

   Esto no es:
   [**ESS**-toh/ **NOH**/ **ESS**]

   • good.

   • bueno.
     [**BWAY**-noh]

   • pretty.

   • bonito.
     [boh-**NEE**-toh]

   • big.

   • grande.
     [**GRAHN**-day]

   • big enough.

   • suficientemente grande.
     [soo-fee-see+enn-tay-**MEN**-tay/ **GRAHN**-day]

   • spacious.

   • espacioso.
     [ess-pah-**SEE+OH**-soh]

   • new.

   • nuevo.
     [**NWAY**-voh]

   • elegant.

   • elegante.
     [ay-lay-**GAHN**-tay]

   • practical.

   • práctico.
     [**PRAHK**-tee-koh]

   • useful.

   • útil.
     [**OO**-teel]

   • of good quality.

   • de buena calidad.
     [day/ **BWAY**-nah/ kah-lee-**DAHD**]

Chapter 13:
Visiting Properties (cont.)

English	Spanish Version & [Phonetic Encoding]

8. This is:
 	
OR
This is not:
 	
• old.
 	
• well constructed.
 	
• almost new.
 	
• included.
 	
• for sale.
	Esto está:
	[**ESS**-toh/ ess-**TAH**]
	OR
	Esto no está:
	[**ESS**-toh/ **NOH**/ ess-**TAH**]
	• viejo.
	  [**VEE+AY**-hoh]
	• bien construído.
	  [**BEE+ENN**/ cons-troo-**EE**-doh]
	• casi nuevo.
	  [**KAH**-see/ **NWAY**-voh]
	• incluído.
	  [een-kloo-**EE**-doh]
	• a la venta.
	  [ah/ lah/ **VENN**-tah]

9. Do you like this one?	¿Le gusta ésta? [lay/ **GOOSE**-tah/ **ESS**-tah♀]
10. Compared to the last one we saw, do you like it more or less?	En comparación a la anterior, ¿le gusta más o menos? [enn/ comb-pah-rah-**SEE+OHN**/ ah/ lah/ ahn-tay-**REE+OR**/ lay/ **GOOSE**-tah/ **MAHS**/ oh/ **MAY**-nohs♀]
11. Would you like to visit it again at another time?	¿Desea verla de nuevo otro día? [day-**SAY**-ah/ **VAIR**-lah/ day/ **NWAY**-voh/ **OH**-troh/ **DEE**-ah♀]
12. Do you want to see other properties?	¿Desea ver otras? [day-**SAY**-ah/ **VAIR**/ **OH**-trahs♀]
13. Let's set up another appointment.	Hagamos otra cita. [ah-**GAH**-mohs/ **OH**-trah/ **SEE**-tah]
14. Let me know if you find something else in the meantime.	Entre tanto dígame si encuentra otra que le interese. [**ENN**-tray/ **TAHN**-toh/ **DEE**-gah-may/ see/ enn-**KWEN**-trah/ **OH**-trah/ kay/ lay/ een-tay-**RAY**-say]
15. I'll keep looking for properties for you.	Voy a seguir buscando propiedades para usted. [**VOY**/ ah/ say-**GEAR**/ boos-**KAHN**-doh/ proh-pee+ay-**DAH**-days/ **PAH**-rah/ oose-**TED**]

Chapter 14:
Making an Offer

English	Spanish Version & [Phonetic Encoding]

CD Two, Track 08

1. Would you like to make an offer?

¿Desea hacer una oferta?
[day-**SAY**-ah/ ah-**SAIR**/ **OO**-nah/ oh-**FAIR**-tah☞]

2. Would you like to place an earnest money deposit?

¿Desea hacer un depósito para iniciar el trato?
[day-**SAY**-ah/ ah-**SAIR**/ oon/ day-**POH**-see-toh/ **PAH**-rah/ ee-nee-**SEE+ARE**/ ell/ **TRAH**-toh☞]

3. If you go up (#) dollars, your monthly payment should only go up approximately (#) dollars.

Si sube a (#) dólares, su pago mensual sólo debe subir como (#) dólares.*
[see/ **SOO**-bay/ ah/ ___/ **DOH**-lah-rays/ soo/ **PAH**-goh/ men-**SOO+AHL**/ **SOH**-loh/ **DAY**-bay/ soo-**BEER**/ **KOH**-moh/ ___/ **DOH**-lah-rays]

4. Once you make an offer and it's accepted, you are obligated to buy it.

Si hace una oferta y la aceptan, usted tiene la obligación de comprarla.
[see/ **AH**-say/ **OO**-nah/ oh-**FAIR**-tah/ ee/ lah/ ah-**SEP**-tahn/ oose-**TED**/ **TEE+AY**-nay/ lah/ oh-blee-gah-**SEE+OHN**/ day/ comb-**PRAHR**-lah]

5. If you change your mind, you can lose your deposit.

Si cambia de opinión, puede perder el dinero del depósito.
[see/ **KAHM**-bee+ah/ day/ oh-pee-**NEE+OHN**/ **PWAY**-day/ pair-**DARE**/ ell/ dee-**NAY**-roh/ dell/ day-**POH**-see-toh]

6. You can withdraw or renegotiate if:

Puede retirar o renegociar la oferta si:
[**PWAY**-day/ rray-tee-**RAHR**/ oh/ rray-nay-goh-**SEE+ARE**/ lah/ oh-**FAIR**-tah/ see]

   • the results of the inspections are not satisfactory.

   • los resultados de las inspecciones no son buenos.
   [lohs/ rray-sool-**TAH**-dohs/ day/ lahs/ eens-pex-**SEE+OH**-nays/ **NOH**/ **SOHN**/ **BWAY**-nohs]

   • your loan is not approved.

   • no aprueban su préstamo.
   [**NOH**/ ah-**PROO+AY**-bahn/ soo/ **PRAYS**-tah-moh]

---

* *See Chapter 4, "Numbers" on page 7.*

Chapter 14:
Making an Offer (cont.)

English	Spanish Version & [Phonetic Encoding]
6. You can withdraw or renegotiate if: (cont.)	Puede retirar o renegociar la oferta si: [**PWAY**-day/ rray-tee-**RAHR**/ oh/ rray-nay-goh-**SEE+ARE**/ lah/ oh-**FAIR**-tah/ see]
• it is contingent on your house selling and it doesn't sell on time.	• depende de la venta de su casa y no se vende a tiempo. [day-**PEN**-day/ day/ lah/ **VENN**-tah/ day/ soo/ **KAH**-sah/ ee/ **NOH**/ say/ **VENN**-day/ ah/ **TEE+EMM**-poh]
• any stipulations in the contract are not met.	• hay alguna estipulación en el contrato que no se cumpla. [**EYE**/ ahl-**GOO**-nah/ ess-tee-poo-lah-**SEE+OHN**/ enn/ ell/ cone-**TRAH**-toh/ kay/ **NOH**/ say/ **KOOM**-plah]
7. How much would you like to offer?	¿Cuánto desea ofrecer? [**KWAN**-toh/ day-**SAY**-ah/ oh-fray-**SAIR**⇧]
8. How much would you like to pay as down payment?	¿Cuándo desea dar de enganche? [**KWAN**-toh/ day-**SAY**-ah/ **DAHR**/ day/ enn-**GAHN**-chay⇧]
9. Your down payment can be:	El enganche puede ser: [ell/ enn-**GAHN**-chay/ **PWAY**-day/ **SAIR**]
• waived.	• eximido. [ex-see-**MEE**-doh]
• (#) percent of the price.	• (#) por ciento del precio.* [___/ por/ **SEE+ENN**-toh/ dell/ **PRAY**-see+oh]
• a specific amount you have in mind.	• una cantidad específica que usted tenga pensada. [**OO**-nah/ kahn-tee-**DAHD**/ ess-pay-**SEE**-fee-kah/ kay/ oose-**TED**/ **TEN**-gah/ pen-**SAH**-dah]
10. I'll pull comparisons for you to look at.	Puedo buscar ejemplos de ofertas a propiedades similares. [**PWAY**-doh/ boos-**CAR**/ ay-**HEM**-plohs/ day/ oh-**FAIR**-tahs/ ah/ proh-pee+ay-**DAH**-days/ see-mee-**LAH**-rays]
11. I need you to come to my office to:	Necesito que venga a mi oficina a: [nay-say-**SEE**-toh/ kay/ **VENN**-gah/ ah/ mee/ oh-fee-**SEE**-nah/ ah/
• review some papers.	• revisar unos papeles. [rray-vee-**SAHR**/ **OO**-nohs/ pah-**PAY**-lays]
• write up your offer.	• hacer su oferta. [ah-**SAIR**/ soo/ oh-**FAIR**-tah]
• sign some papers.	• firmar unos papeles. [fear-**MAHR**/ **OO**-nohs/ pah-**PAY**-lays]

---

* *See Chapter 4, "Numbers" on page 7.*

Chapter 14:
Making an Offer (cont.)

English	Spanish Version & [Phonetic Encoding]
12. When you come, bring: **OR** When you go, bring:	Cuando venga, traiga: [**KWAN**-doh/ **VENN**-gah/ **TRY**-gah] **OR** Cuando vaya, traiga: [**KWAN**-doh/ **VAH**-yah/ **TRY**-gah]
• your spouse.	• a su cónyuge*. [ah/ soo/ **CONE**-you-hay]
• whoever you want to be part of the contract.	• a quien quiera que sea parte del contrato. [ah/ **KEE+ENN**/ **KEY+AY**-rah/ kay/ **SAY**-ah/ **PAR**-tay/ dell/ cone-**TRAH**-toh]
• an interpreter.	• a un traductor. [ah/ oon/ trah-duke-**TOHR**]
• your social security card.	• su tarjeta de seguro social. [soo/ tar-**HAY**-tah/ day/ say-**GOO**-roh/ soh-see+**AHL**]
• your driver's license.	• su licencia de conducir. [soo/ lee-**SEN**-see+ah/ day/ cone-doo-**SEER**]
• the certified check for *(amount)*.	• el cheque certificado por *(#)* dólares.† [ell/ **CHAY**-kay/ sair-tee-fee-**KAH**-doh/ por/ ___/ **DOH**-lah-rays]
• your checkbook.	• su chequera. [soo/ chay-**KAY**-rah]
• the prequalification letter.	• la carta de pre-calificación. [lah/ **CAR**-tah/ day/ pray-kah-lee-fee-kah-**SEE+OHN**]
• the balance of the down payment.	• el resto del enganche. [ell/ **RRAYS**-toh/ dell/ enn-**GAHN**-chay]
• all of these documents. (point to list)	• todos estos documentos. [**TOH**-dohs/ **ESS**-tohs/ doh-koo-**MEN**-tohs]
13. You will need to make a deposit of *(amount)* with your offer.	Va a tener que dar un depósito de *(#)* dólares con la oferta. [**VAH**/ ah/ tay-**NAIR**/ kay/ **DAR**/ oon/ day-**POH**-see-toh/ day/ ___/ **DOH**-lah-rays/ cone/ lah/ oh-**FAIR**-tah]
14. We accept cash. **OR** We don't accept cash.	Aceptamos efectivo. [ah-sep-**TAH**-mohs/ ay-feck-**TEE**-voh] **OR** No aceptamos efectivo. [**NOH**/ ah-sep-**TAH**-mohs/ ay-feck-**TEE**-voh]
15. Your offer could be accepted or denied.	Pueden aceptar o rechazar su oferta. [**PWAY**-den/ ah-sep-**TAR**/ oh/ rray-chah-**SAHR**/ soo/ oh-**FAIR**-tah]

* See *"Appendix A: Cultural Notes"* on page 63.
† See Chapter 4, "Numbers" on page 7.

Chapter 14:
Making an Offer (cont.)

English	Spanish Version & [Phonetic Encoding]
16. If they accept it and the home inspection is satisfactory:	Si la aceptan y la inspección es satisfactoria: [see/ lah/ ah-**SEP**-tahn/ ee/ lah/ eens-pex-**SEE+OHN**/ **ESS**/ sah-tees-fack-**TOH**-ree+ah]
• you will sign a purchase and sale agreement.	• tiene que firmar un acuerdo de compra-venta. [**TEE+AY**-nay/ kay/ fear-**MAHR**/ oon/ ah-**KWAIR**-doh/ day/ comb-prah-**VENN**-tah]
• they will sign it too.	• ellos también lo tienen que firmar. [**AY**-yohs/ tahm-**BEE+ENN**/ loh/ **TEE+AY**-nen/ kay/ fear-**MAHR**]
• you will need to provide a certified check for (#) percent of the price on the agreement.	• tiene que dar un cheque certificado por el (#) por ciento del precio en el acuerdo.* [**TEE+AY**-nay/ kay/ **DAR**/ oon/ **CHAY**-kay/ sair-tee-fee-**KAH**-doh/ por/ ell/ ___/ por/ **SEE+ENN**-toh/ dell/ **PRAY**-see+oh/ enn/ ell/ ah-**KWAIR**-doh]
17. The purchase and sale agreeement outlines the terms of the contract.	El acuerdo de compra-venta especifica los términos del contrato. [ell/ ah-**KWAIR**-doh/ day/ comb-prah-**VENN**-tah/ ess-pay-see-**FEE**-kah/ lohs/ **TAIR**-mee-nohs/ dell/ cone-**TRAH**-toh]
18. I'm going to talk to them.	Voy a hablar con ellos. [**VOY**/ ah/ ah-**BLAHR**/ cone/ **AY**-yohs]
19. I'm going to present your offer to them.	Voy a presentar su oferta. [**VOY**/ ah/ pray-sen-**TAR**/ soo/ oh-**FAIR**-tah]
20. They should respond before *(day of the week or date)*.	Deben responder antes del *(day of the week or date)*.† [**DAY**-ben/ rrays-pohn-**DAIR**/ **AHN**-tays/ dell/ ___]
21. I will let you know what they say as soon as I can.	Yo le aviso qué responden cuanto antes. [**YOH**/ lay/ ah-**VEE**-soh/ **KAY**/ rrays-**POHN**-den/ **KWAN**-toh/ **AHN**-tays]
22. Good luck.	Buena suerte. [**BWAY**-nah/ **SWAIR**-tay]
23. I hope it works for you.	Espero que le vaya bien. [ess-**PAY**-roh/ kay/ lay/ **VAH**-yah/ **BEE+ENN**]

---

* *See Chapter 4, "Numbers" on page 7.*
† *See "Appendix F: Announcing Dates and Times" on page 67.*

Chapter 15:
Seller's Response

English	Spanish Version & [Phonetic Encoding]

CD Two, Track 09

1. The sellers want:

  Los vendedores desean:
  [lohs/ venn-day-**DOH**-rays/ day-**SAY**-ahn]

   • more money.

   • más dinero.
   [**MAHS**/ dee-**NAY**-roh]

   • (#) dollars.

   • (#) dólares *
   [___/ **DOH**-lah-rays]

   • to see a copy of your prequalification letter.

   • ver una copia de su carta de pre-calificación.
   [**VAIR**/ **OO**-nah/ **KOH**-pee+ah/ day/ soo/ **CAR**-tah/ day/ pray-kah-lee-fee-kah-**SEE+OHN**]

   • to share the closing costs with you.

   • compartir los costos del cierre con usted.
   [comb-pahr-**TEER**/ lohs/ **KOHS**-tohs/ dell/ **SEE+AY**-rray/ cone/ oose-**TED**]

   • to close on this date. (point to calendar)

   • hacer el cierre este día.
   [ah-**SAIR**/ ell/ **SEE+AY**-rray/ **ESS**-tay/ **DEE**-ah]

2. They want you to pay for:

  Ellos desean que usted pague:
  [**AY**-yohs/ day-**SAY**-ahn/ kay/ oose-**TED**/ **PAH**-gay]

OR

I'll tell them you want them to pay for:

OR

Voy a decirles que usted desea que ellos paguen:
[**VOY**/ ah/ day-**SEER**-lays/ kay/ oose-**TED**/ day-**SAY**-ah/ kay/ **AY**-yohs/ **PAH**-gain]

   • (*amount*) of the closing costs.

   • (#) dólares de los costos del cierre.
   [___/ **DOH**-lah-rays/ day/ lohs/ **KOHS**-tohs/ dell/ **SEE+AY**-rray]

   • the buyer's closing costs.

   • los costos de cierre del comprador.
   [lohs/ **KOHS**-tohs/ day/ **SEE+AY**-rray/ dell/ comb-prah-**DOHR**]

   • the seller's closing costs.

   • los costos de cierre del vendedor.
   [lohs/ **KOHS**-tohs/ day/ **SEE+AY**-rray/ dell/ venn-day-**DOHR**]

   • the property appraisal.

   • el avalúo de la propiedad.
   [ell/ ah-vah-**LOO**-oh/ day/ lah/ proh-pee+ay-**DAHD**]

   • the house inspection.

   • la inspección de la casa.
   [lah/ eens-pex-**SEE+OHN**/ day/ lah/ **KAH**-sah]

   • the termite inspection.

   • la inspección de termitas.
   [lah/ eens-pex-**SEE+OHN**/ day/ tair-**MEE**-tahs]

* *See Chapter 4, "Numbers" on page 7.*

Chapter 15:
Seller's Response (cont.)

English	Spanish Version & [Phonetic Encoding]
2. They want you to pay for: (cont.)	Ellos desean que usted pague: [**AY**-yohs/ day-**SAY**-ahn/ kay/ oose-**TED**/ **PAH**-gay]
OR I'll tell them you want them to pay for: (cont.)	OR Voy a decirles que usted desea que ellos paguen: [**VOY**/ ah/ day-**SEER**-lays/ kay/ oose-**TED**/ day-**SAY**-ah/ kay/ **AY**-yohs/ **PAH**-gain]
• the flood inspection.	• la inspección de inundación. [lah/ eens-pex-**SEE+OHN**/ day/ ee-noon-dah-**SEE+OHN**]
• the survey.	• el peritaje topográfico. [ell/ pay-ree-**TAH**-hay/ toh-poh-**GRAH**-fee-koh]
• the repairs.	• las reparaciones. [lahs/ rray-pah-rah-**SEE+OH**-nays]
• the homeowner's insurance.	• el seguro de la propiedad. [ell/ say-**GOO**-roh/ day/ lah/ proh-pee+ay-**DAHD**]
• the legal fees.	• las cuotas legales. [lahs/ **KWOH**-tahs/ lay-**GAH**-lays]
3. All closing costs are negotiable.	Todos los costos de cierre son negociables. [**TOH**-dohs/ lohs/ **KOHS**-tohs/ day/ **SEE+AY**-rray/ **SOHN**/ nay-goh-**SEE+AH**-blays]
4. The buyer usually pays for this. (point to applicable fees from list)	El comprador generalmente paga esto. [ell/ comb-prah-**DOHR**/ gay-nay-rahl-**MEN**-tay/ **PAH**-gah/ **ESS**-toh]
5. The seller usually pays for this. (point to applicable fees from list)	El vendedor generalmente paga esto. [ell/ venn-day-**DOHR**/ gay-nay-rahl-**MEN**-tay/ **PAH**-gah/ **ESS**-toh]
6. You need to give some earnest money deposit.	Tiene que dar un depósito para iniciar el trato. [**TEE+AY**-nay/ kay/ **DAR**/ oon/ day-**POH**-see-toh/ **PAH**-rah/ ee-nee-**SEE+ARE**/ ell/ **TRAH**-toh]
7. They want (#) dollars as deposit.	Piden (#) dólares de depósito.* [**PEE**-den/ ___/ **DOH**-lah-rays/ day/ day-**POH**-see-toh]
8. It will be held until the closing.	Se va a guardar hasta que se cierre el trato. [say/ **VAH**/ ah/ goo+are-**DAHR**/ **AHS**-tah/ kay/ say/ **SEE+AY**-rray/ ell/ **TRAH**-toh]

* *See Chapter 4, "Numbers" on page 7.*

Chapter 15:
Seller's Response (cont.)

English	Spanish Version & [Phonetic Encoding]
9. It will be held by:	Lo va a guardar: [loh/ **VAH**/ ah/ goo+are-**DAHR**]
• the seller's broker.	• el agente del vendedor. [ell/ ah-**HEN**-tay/ dell/ venn-day-**DOHR**]
• the title company.	• la compañía que hace el título. [lah/ comb-pah-**NYEE**-ah/ kay/ **AH**-say/ ell/ **TEE**-too-loh]
• the attorney for the closing.	• el abogado del cierre. [ell/ ah-boh-**GAH**-doh/ dell/ **SEE+AY**-rray]
10. It is helpful for both parties.	Es bueno para ambas partes. [**ESS**/ **BWAY**-noh/ **PAH**-rah/ **AHM**-bahs/ **PAR**-tays]
11. It will show them that you are serious about the deal.	Eso les demuestra su verdadero interés en la compra. [**AY**-soh/ lays/ day-**MWAYS**-trah/ soo/ vair-dah-**DAY**-roh/ een-tay-**RAYS**/ enn/ lah/ **COMB**-prah]
12. The seller keeps it if you break the deal without just cause.	El vendedor se queda con él si usted deshace el negocio sin una causa justificada. [ell/ venn-day-**DOHR**/ say/ **KAY**-dah/ cone/ **ELL**/ see/ oose-**TED**/ days-**AH**-say/ ell/ nay-**GOH**-see+oh/ seen/ **OO**-nah/ **COW**-sah/ hoos-tee-fee-**KAH**-dah]
13. It can be applied to the price of the property.	Usted puede usar ese dinero como parte del pago de la propiedad. [oose-**TED**/ **PWAY**-day/ oo-**SAR**/ **AY**-say/ dee-**NAY**-roh/ **KOH**-moh/ **PAR**-tay/ dell/ **PAH**-goh/ day/ lah/ proh-pee+ay-**DAHD**]
14. You can pay with:	Puede pagar con: [**PWAY**-day/ pah-**GAR**/ cone]
• a personal check.	• un cheque personal. [oon/ **CHAY**-kay/ pair-soh-**NAHL**]
• a money order.	• un giro. [oon/ **HEE**-roh]
• cash.	• efectivo. [ay-feck-**TEE**-voh]
• a cashier's check.	• un cheque de caja. [oon/ **CHAY**-kay/ day/ **KAH**-hah]
15. We will put a "sale pending" sign outside.	Vamos a poner un letrero de "Sale Pending" afuera. [**VAH**-mohs/ ah/ poh-**NAIR**/ oon/ lay-**TRAY**-roh/ day/ *SALE*/ *PENDING*/ ah-**FWAY**-rah]

Chapter 15:
Seller's Response (cont.)

English	Spanish Version & [Phonetic Encoding]
16. They will probably stop showing the property to other possible buyers in the meantime.	Tal vez dejen de mostrar la propiedad a otros posibles compradores mientras tanto. [tahl-**VACE**/ **DAY**-hen/ day/ mohs-**TRAHR**/ lah/ proh-pee+ay-**DAHD**/ ah/ **OH**-trohs/ poh-**SEE**-blays/ comb-prah-**DOH**-rays/ **MEE+ENN**-trahs/ **TAHN**-toh]
17. However, the property remains on the market until closing.	Sin embargo, la propiedad sigue en el mercado hasta el día del cierre. [seen/ emm-**BAHR**-goh/ lah/ proh-pee+ay-**DAHD**/ **SEE**-gay/ enn/ ell/ mair-**KAH**-doh/ **AHS**-tah/ ell/ **DEE**-ah/ dell/ **SEE+AY**-rray]
18. They will give you first choice if another buyer comes up.	Ellos van a darle prioridad a usted si otro comprador se interesa en la propiedad. [**AY**-yohs/ **VAHN**/ ah/ **DAHR**-lay/ pree+oh-ree-**DAHD**/ ah/ oose-**TED**/ see/ **OH**-troh/ comb-prah-**DOHR**/ say/ een-tay-**RAY**-sah/ enn/ lah/ proh-pee+ay-**DAHD**]
19. If that happens and the buyer offers more money, you can change your offer.	Si eso pasa y el otro comprador ofrece más dinero, usted puede cambiar su oferta. [see/ **AY**-soh/ **PAH**-sah/ ee/ ell/ **OH**-troh/ comb-prah-**DOHR**/ oh-**FRAY**-say/ **MAHS**/ dee-**NAY**-roh/ oose-**TED**/ **PWAY**-day/ kahm-**BEE+ARE**/ soo/ oh-**FAIR**-tah]
20. I have good news for you.	Le tengo buenas noticias. [lay/ **TEN**-goh/ **BWAY**-nahs/ noh-**TEE**-see+ahs]
21. They accepted your offer.	Aceptaron su oferta. [ah-sep-**TAH**-rohn/ soo/ oh-**FAIR**-tah]
22. Congratulations!	¡Felicitaciones! [fay-lee-see-tah-**SEE+OH**-nays]
23. I'm sorry.	Lo siento. [loh/ **SEE+ENN**-toh]
24. They didn't accept your offer.	No aceptaron su oferta. [**NOH**/ ah-sep-**TAH**-rohn/ soo/ oh-**FAIR**-tah]
25. They counter-offered.	Hicieron una contra oferta. [ee-**SEE+AY**-rohn/ **OO**-nah/ **CONE**-trah/ oh-**FAIR**-tah]
26. Do you accept it?	¿La acepta? [lah/ ah-**SEP**-tah⇧]

Chapter 15:
Seller's Response (cont.)

English	Spanish Version & [Phonetic Encoding]
27. You can reject it.	Usted puede rechazarla. [oose-**TED**/ **PWAY**-day/ rray-chah-**SAR**-lah]
28. You can make a counter offer.	Usted puede hacer una contra oferta. [oose-**TED**/ **PWAY**-day/ ah-**SAIR**/ **OO**-nah/ **CONE**-trah/ oh-**FAIR**-tah]
29. What would you like to change in order to accept it?	¿Qué desea cambiar para aceptarla? [**KAY**/ day-**SAY**-ah/ kahm-**BEE+ARE**/ **PAH**-rah/ ah-sep-**TAHR**-lah⇧]
30. They insist on their demands.	Ellos insisten en sus términos. [**AY**-yohs/ een-**SEES**-tayn/ enn/ soos/ **TAIR**-mee-nohs]
31. Think about it and let me know what you have decided.	Piénselo y dígame qué decidió. [**PEE+ENN**-say-loh/ ee/ **DEE**-gah-may/ **KAY**/ day-see-**DEE+OH**]

Chapter 16:
Executing the Purchase and Sale Agreement

English	Spanish Version & [Phonetic Encoding]

Unit A: Before Negotiating the Purchase and Sale Agreement
CD Two, Track 10

1. We have the results from the inspection for:
   Ya recibimos los resultados de la inspección de:
   [**YAH**/ rray-see-**BEE**-mohs/ lohs/ rray-sool-**TAH**-dohs/ day/ lah/ eens-pex-**SEE+OHN**/ day]

   • the property.
       • la propiedad.
         [lah/ proh-pee+ay-**DAHD**]

   • termites.
       • termitas.
         [tair-**MEE**-tahs]

   • lead based paint.
       • pintura a base de plomo.
         [peen-**TOO**-rah/ ah/ **BAH**-say/ day/ **PLOH**-moh]

   • radon gas.
       • gas radón.
         [**GAS**/ rah-**DOHN**]

   • asbestos.
       • asbesto.
         [ahs-**BAYS**-toh]

   • flooding.
       • inundación.
         [ee-noon-dah-**SEE+OHN**]

2. They are good.
   Son buenos.
   [**SOHN**/ **BWAY**-nohs]

   OR
   OR

   They are not good.
   No son buenos.
   [**NOH**/ **SOHN**/ **BWAY**-nohs]

3. The results of the report show:
   Los resultados del reporte muestran que:
   [lohs/ rray-sool-**TAH**-dohs/ dell/ rray-**POR**-tay/ **MWAYS**-trahn/ kay]

   • this has to be repaired. (point)
       • hay que reparar esto.
         [**EYE**/ kay/ rray-pah-**RAHR**/ **ESS**-toh]

   • this has to be fixed. (point)
       • hay que arreglar esto.
         [**EYE**/ kay/ ah-rray-**GLAHR**/ **ESS**-toh]

   • this has to be replaced. (point)
       • hay que cambiar esto.
         [**EYE**/ kay/ kahm-**BEE+ARE**/ **ESS**-toh]

   • this doesn't work. (point)
       • esto no funciona.
         [**ESS**-toh/ **NOH**/ foon-**SEE+OH**-nah]

   • there's structural damage here. (point)
       • hay daño en la estructura aquí.
         [**EYE**/ **DAH**-nyoh/ enn/ lah/ ess-trook-**TOO**-rah/ ah-**KEY**]

   • there's termite damage here. (point)
       • hay daño de termitas aquí.
         [**EYE**/ **DAH**-nyoh/ day/ tair-**MEE**-tahs/ ah-**KEY**]

Chapter 16:
Executing the Purchase and Sale Agreement (cont.)

English	Spanish Version & [Phonetic Encoding]

Unit B: Negotiating the Purchase and Sale Agreement
CD Two, Track 11

1. The current owners will move out on this date. (point to calendar)

   Los dueños se van a mudar este día.
   [lohs/ **DWAY**-nohs/ say/ **VAHN**/ ah/ moo-**DAHR**/ **ESS**-tay/ **DEE**-ah]

2. You may move in on this date. (point to calendar)

   Usted se puede mudar a partir de este día.
   [oose-**TED**/ say/ **PWAY**-day/ moo-**DAHR**/ ah/ par-**TEER**/ day/ **ESS**-tay/ **DEE**-ah]

3. This is the purchase and sale agreement. (point)

   Este es el acuerdo de compra-venta.
   [**ESS**-tay/ **ESS**/ ell/ ah-**KWAIR**-doh/ day/ comb-prah-**VENN**-tah]

4. Write your name:

   Escriba su nombre:
   [ess-**KREE**-bah/ soo/ **NOME**-bray]

   OR
   Sign:

   OR
   Firme:
   [**FEAR**-may]

   OR
   Put your initials:

   OR
   Ponga sus iniciales:
   [**PONE**-gah/ soos/ ee-nee-**SEE+AH**-lays]

   • here. (point)

   • aquí.
   [ah-**KEY**]

   • where the X appears.

   • donde está la equis.
   [**DOAN**-day/ ess-**TAH**/ lah/ **AY**-keys]

   • where it's highlighted.

   • donde está resaltado.
   [**DOAN**-day/ ess-**TAH**/ rray-sahl-**TAH**-doh]

Unit C: After the Purchase and Sale Agreement Has Been Signed
CD Two, Track 12

1. Your lender will require home owner's insurance.

   Su prestamista va a exigirle tener seguro de propietario de vivienda.
   [soo/ prays-tah-**MEES**-tah/ **VAH**/ ah/ ex-see-**HERE**-lay/ tay-**NAIR**/ say-**GOO**-roh/ day/ proh-pee+ay-**TAH**-ree+oh/ day/ vee-**VEE+ENN**-dah]

2. Do you already have an insurance company?

   ¿Ya tiene compañía de seguros?
   [**YAH**/ **TEE+AY**-nay/ comb-pah-**NYEE**-ah/ day/ say-**GOO**-rohs⇗]

Chapter 16:
Executing the Purchase and Sale Agreement (cont.)

English	Spanish Version & [Phonetic Encoding]

Unit C: After the Purchase and Sale Agreement Has Been Signed (cont.)

3. Here are a couple of choices. (give business cards)

Estas son un par de opciones.
[**ESS**-tahs/ **SOHN**/ oon/ **PAHR**/ day/ ohp-**SEE+OH**-nays]

4. They speak Spanish.

<u>OR</u>

They don't speak Spanish.

Hablan español.
[**AH**-blahn/ ess-pah-**NYOHL**]

<u>OR</u>

No hablan español.
[**NOH**/ **AH**-blahn/ ess-pah-**NYOHL**]

5. We need to schedule a final walkthrough before the closing.

Tenemos que ponernos de acuerdo para la última visita antes del cierre.
[tay-**NAY**-mohs/ kay/ poh-**NAIR**-nohs/ day/ ah-**KWAIR**-doh/ **PAH**-rah/ lah/ **OOL**-tee-mah/ vee-**SEE**-tah/ **AHN**-tays/ dell/ **SEE+AY**-rray]

Chapter 17:
Before the Closing

English	Spanish Version & [Phonetic Encoding]

CD Two, Track 13

1. I will call and schedule the appointment for:

   Voy a llamar para hacer la cita para:
   [**VOY**/ ah/ yah-**MAHR**/ **PAH**-rah/ ah-**SAIR**/ lah/ **SEE**-tah/ **PAH**-rah]

   <u>OR</u>

   You need to schedule the appointment for:

   <u>OR</u>

   Tiene que hacer la cita para:
   [**TEE+AY**-nay/ kay/ ah-**SAIR**/ lah/ **SEE**-tah/ **PAH**-rah]

   - the house inspection.
     - la inspección de la casa.
       [lah/ eens-pex-**SEE+OHN**/ day/ lah/ **KAH**-sah]
   - purchasing homeowner's insurance.
     - obtener el seguro de la propiedad.
       [ohb-tay-**NAIR**/ ell/ say-**GOO**-roh/ day/ lah/ proh-pee+ay-**DAHD**]
   - the loan approval.
     - la aprobación del préstamo.
       [lah/ ah-proh-bah-**SEE+OHN**/ dell/ **PRAYS**-tah-moh]

2. You must bring:

   Tiene que traer:
   [**TEE+AY**-nay/ kay/ trah-**AIR**]

   - your social security card.
     - su tarjeta de seguro social.
       [soo/ tar-**HAY**-tah/ day/ say-**GOO**-roh/ soh-**SEE+AHL**]
   - your driver's license.
     - su licencia de conducir.
       [soo/ lee-**SEN**-see+ah/ day/ cone-doo-**SEER**]
   - a photo ID.
     - una identificación con foto.
       [**OO**-nah/ ee-den-tee-fee-kah-**SEE+OHN**/ cone/ **FOH**-toh]
   - the certified check for *(amount)*.
     - el cheque certificado por *(#)* dólares.*
       [ell/ **CHAY**-kay/ sair-tee-fee-**KAH**-doh/ por/ ___/ **DOH**-lah-rays]
   - your checkbook.
     - su chequera.
       [soo/ chay-**KAY**-rah]
   - all of these documents. (provide list)
     - todos estos documentos.
       [**TOH**-dohs/ **ESS**-tohs/ doh-koo-**MEN**-tohs]
   - proof of your homeowner's insurance.
     - prueba del seguro de la propiedad.
       [**PROO+AY**-bah/ dell/ say-**GOO**-roh/ day/ lah/ proh-pee+ay-**DAHD**]

---

* *See Chapter 4, "Numbers" on page 7.*

Chapter 17:
Before the Closing (cont).

English	Spanish Version & [Phonetic Encoding]
3. Write the check for *(amount)*.	Haga el cheque por *(#)* dólares.* [**AH**-gah/ ell/ **CHAY**-kay/ por/ ___/ **DOH**-lah-rays]
4. Write the check payable to *(name or company)*.	Haga el cheque a nombre de *(name or company)*. [**AH**-gah/ ell/ **CHAY**-kay/ ah/ **NOME**-bray/ day/ ___]

---

* See Chapter 4, "Numbers" on page 7.

Chapter 18:
During the Closing

English	Spanish Version & [Phonetic Encoding]

CD Two, Track 14

1. Write your name:

   OR
   Sign:

   OR
   Put your initials:

   - here. (point)

   - where the X appears.

   - where it's highlighted.

Escriba su nombre:
[ess-**KREE**-bah/ soo/ **NOME**-bray]

OR
Firme:
[**FEAR**-may]

OR
Ponga sus iniciales:
[**PONE**-gah/ soos/ ee-nee-**SEE+AH**-lays]

- aquí.
  [ah-**KEY**]
- donde está la equis.
  [**DOAN**-day/ ess-**TAH**/ lah/ **AY**-keys]
- donde está resaltado.
  [**DOAN**-day/ ess-**TAH**/ rray-sahl-**TAH**-doh]

2. Here are your new keys.

Estas son sus nuevas llaves.
[**ESS**-tahs/ **SOHN**/ soos/ **NWAY**-vahs/ **YAH**-vays]

3. Here is a little gift for you.

Este es un regalito para usted.
[**ESS**-tay/ **ESS**/ oon/ rray-gah-**LEE**-toh/ **PAH**-rah/ oose-**TED**]

4. Congratulations!

¡Felicitaciones!
[fay-lee-see-tah-**SEE+OH**-nays]

5. You own a new home!

¡Ya es dueño de una casa!
[**YAH**/ **ESS**/ **DWAY**-nyoh/ day/ **OO**-nah/ **KAH**-sah]

Appendix A:
Cultural Notes

SIGNATURES:
When Latin Americans are asked to "write" their name, they typically write or print it in legible fashion. But when they are asked to "sign" their name, they often produce an indecipherable, personalized flurry of pen strokes that cannot be read by anyone but the person signing.

REALTOR/REALTY AGENT (*Agente de Bienes Raíces*):
The most common word for "realtor" or "realty agent" is *agente de bienes raíces*. Other terms are *agente de finca raíz* [ah-**HEN**-tay/ day/ **FEEN**-kah/ rrah-**EESE**].

HOME (*Casa*):
The most common word for "home" is *casa*, even though the literal translation would be *hogar* [oh-**GAHR**]. *Casa* means house" but is also used when referring to "apartment" *departamento* [day-par-tah-**MEN**-toh] or *apartamento* [ah-par-tah-**MEN**-toh] or any other living arrangement?? *vivienda* [vee-**VEE+ENN**-dah]

GARDEN/YARD (*Jardín*):
The most common word for "garden" or "yard" is *jardín*. It may be used to refer to the "backyard" or "frontyard" or simply a strip of greenery, but it does not convey the same meaning as the concept of "vegetable garden," which is *huerta*.

RENT (*Rentar*):
The most common word for "rent, to" is *rentar*. Other terms are *alquilar* [ahl-kee-**LAHR**] and *arrendar* [ah-rren-**DAHR**]

FLOORS/STORIES (*Pisos*):
The most common word for "floors" is *pisos*. Another term is *plantas* [**PLAHN**-tahs].

BEDROOM (*Recámara*):
The most common word for "bedroom" among Mexicans is *recámara*. Other countries may use *cuarto* [**KWAHR**-toh], *habitación* [ah-bee-tah-**SEE+OHN**], *pieza* [**PEE+AY**-sah], *alcoba* [ahl-**KOH**-bah].

POOL (*Alberca*):
The most common word for "pool" among Mexicans is *alberca*. Other countries may use *piscina* [pee-**SEE**-nah].

LAWN/GRASS (*Pasto*):
The most common word for "lawn" is *pasto*. Other terms are *césped* [**SAYS**-ped], *prado* [**PRAH**-doh], *hierba* [**YAIR**-bah], *grama* [**GRAH**-mah]

SHOWER (*Regadera*):
The most common word for "shower" is *regadera*. Another term is *ducha* [**DOO**-chah].

BATHROOM SINK (*Lavamanos*):
The most common word for "bathroom sink" is *lavamanos*. Another term is *lavabo* [lah-**VAH**-boh].

KITCHEN SINK (*Fregadero*):
The most common word for "kitchen sink" is *fregadero*. Another term is *lavaplatos* [lah-vah-**PLAH**-tohs].

NEIGHBORHOOD/SUBDIVISION (*Vecindario*):
The most common word for "neighborhood" or "subdivision" is *vecindario*. Other terms are *colonia* [koh-**LOH**-nee+ah], *fraccionamiento* [frax-see+oh-nah-**MEE+ENN**-toh], *barrio* [**BAH**-rree+oh], *desarrollo urbano* [day-sah-**RROH**-yoh/ oor-**BAH**-noh], *conjunto* [cone-**HOON**-toh], *complejo residencial* [comb-**PLAY**-hoh/ rray-see-den-**SEE+AHL**].

SPOUSE (*Cónyuge*):
The term for "spouse" is *cónyuge*, however, other terms are more commonly used when referring to each specific gender that would correspond to the English terms "husband" *esposo* [ess-**POH**-soh] and "wife" *esposa* [ess-**POH**-sah].

Appendix B:
Spanish Alphabet

Spanish Letter	Pronunciation		
A	**AH**		
B	**BAY**		
C	**SAY**		
D	**DAY**		
E	**AY**		
F	**AY**-fay		
G	**HAY**		
H	**AH**-chay		
I	**EE**		
J	**HOH**-tah		
K	**KAH**		
L	**AY**-lay		
M	**AY**-may		
N	**AY**-nay		
Ñ	**AY**-nyay		
O	**OH**		
P	**PAY**		
Q	**KOO**		
R	**AY**-ray		
S	**AY**-say		
T	**TAY**		
U	**OO**		
V	**VAY**		
W	**DOH**-blay/ **OO**	*OR*	**DOH**-blay/ **VAY**
X	**AY**-keys		
Y	**EE**/ **GREE+AY**-gah	*OR*	**YAY**
Z	**SAY**-tah		

Appendix C:
Spanish Surname System

"The Curious Case of Two Last Names"

A very common mistake made by non-Hispanics is the incorrect identification of Latin American surnames. In order to avoid this mistake, study the information below.

In Latin America, most people are given two first names at birth, and *everyone* receives two last names. There is no such thing as a middle name.

When deciphering a person's last name on a document, you should seek out the first of the two last names because that is the name used for legal purposes and banking transactions.

EXAMPLE: Is this woman's last name Delgado or Gómez?

María Josefina <u>Delgado</u> Gómez

Answer: We know that María and Josefina are her two first names. In the case of the two last names, only Delgado, which was her father's family name, counts. In other words, if you met this woman at a party, she would introduce herself as María Delgado or Josefina Delgado. She is not Ms. Gómez, which was her mother's family name.

Can you correctly identify the last name of the following people?

1. Roberto Moreno Durán
2. María Elena Solano Ruiz
3. Eduardo Adolfo Suárez Pérez
4. Claudia Patricia Barbosa Acero
5. Camilo Andrés Castro Aguirre
6. Mónica Jiménez Torres

Answers:
1. Moreno
2. Solano
3. Suárez
4. Barbosa
5. Castro
6. Jiménez

Appendix D:
Money Issues

Stating an amount of money in Spanish is very similar to the way that one would state it in English. Just like in English, there are two ways to express an amount of money—with the words "dollars" and "cents" and without them. Both formats are correct, but you will minimize confusion if you opt for the format that *does* use the words "dollars" and "cents."

Take a look at the following examples:

Example #1

$ 25.30   veinticinco **dólares**, treinta **centavos** (twenty five **dollars**, thirty **cents**)

<u>OR</u>

veinticinco, treinta (twenty five, thirty)

Example #2

$ 99.50   noventa y nueve **dólares**, cincuenta **centavos** (ninety nine **dollars**, fifty **cents**)

<u>OR</u>

noventa y nueve, cincuenta (ninety nine, fifty)

Example #3

$1,345.89   mil tresceintos cuarenta y cinco **dólares**, ochenta y nueve **centavos** (one thousand, three hundred and forty five **dollars**, eighty nine **cents**)

<u>OR</u>

mil, tresceintos cuarenta y cinco, ochenta y nueve (one thousand, three hundred and forty five, eighty nine)

Appendix E:
Announcing Dates and Times

Months

1.	January	enero [ay-**NAY**-roh]
2.	February	febrero [fay-**BRAY**-roh]
3.	March	marzo [**MAR**-soh]
4.	April	abril [ah-**BREEL**]
5.	May	mayo [**MAH**-yoh]
6.	June	junio [**HOO**-nee+oh]
7.	July	julio [**HOO**-lee+oh]
8.	August	agosto [ah-**GOHS**-toh]
9.	September	septiembre [sep-**TEE+EMM**-bray]
10.	October	octubre [oak-**TOO**-bray]
11.	November	noviembre [noh-**VEE+EMM**-bray]
12.	December	diciembre [dee-**SEE+EMM**-bray]

Days

1.	Sunday	domingo [doh-**MEEN**-goh]
2.	Monday	lunes [**LOO**-nays]
3.	Tuesday	martes [**MAR**-tays]
4.	Wednesday	miércoles [**MEE+AIR**-koh-lays]
5.	Thursday	jueves [**HWAY**-vays]
6.	Friday	viernes [**VEE+AIR**-nays]
7.	Saturday	sábado [**SAH**-bah-doh]

Appendix E:
Announcing Dates and Times (cont.)

How to Give Dates

Spanish-speakers report calendar dates in a slightly different manner than we do in English. The most important difference is that the day of the month is given before the name of the month (U.S. Military style).

While in English we would say "January 15, 1972" (1/15/72), a Spanish-speaker would say "the 15th of January of 1972" (15/1/72).

·Examples:	ENGLISH	SPANISH
	December 25, 1943	25 de diciembre de 1943 (veinte y cinco de diciembre de mil novecientos cuarenta y tres)
	May 5, 1970	5 de mayo de 1970 (cinco de mayo de mil novecientos setenta)

How to announce a set time

For telling **AT** what time something happens, use "*A la (time)...*" (for at one o'clock and its parts) or "*A las (time)...*"(for all other times). For example:

| At one o'clock... | A la una... | ah/ lah/ OO-nah |
| At two o'clock... | A las dos... | ah/ lahs/ DOHS |

1. You need to come on: *(day of the week)*.

    Necesita venir el: *(day of the week)*.
        [nay-say-**SEE**-tah/ vay-**NEER**/ ell/ ___]

2. You need to come on: *(date)*.

    Necesita venir el: *(date)*.
        [nay-say-**SEE**-tah/ vay-**NEER**/ ell/ ___]

3. You need to come at: *(time)*.

    Necesita venir a la(s): *(time)*.
        [nay-say-**SEE**-tah/ vay-**NEER**/ ah/ lah(s)/ ___]

4. They will be ready at: *(time)*.

    Van a estar listos a la(s): *(time)*.
        [**VAHN**/ ah/ ess-**TAR**/ **LEES**-tohs/ ah/ lah(s)/ ___]

Appendix F:
Giving Directions

Go:

OR

Turn:

OR

Continue:

OR

Pass:

OR

Cross:

OR

It is:

- across from

- after

- avenue

- before

- beside

- block

- corner

- east

- highway

- near

- next to

- north

- on the left

Vaya:
  [**VAH**-yah]

OR

Voltee:
  [vohl-**TAY**-ay]

OR

Continúe:
  [cone-tee-**NOO**-ay]

OR

Pase:
  [**PAH**-say]

OR

Cruce:
  [**KROO**-say]

OR

Está:
  [ess-**TAH**]
  - al frente de
    [ahl/ **FRAIN**-tay/ day]
  - después de
    [days-**PWAYS**/ day]
  - avenida
    [ah-vay-**NEE**-dah]
  - antes de
    [**AHN**-tays/ day]
  - al lado de
    [ahl/ **LAH**-doh/ day]
  - cuadra
    [**KWAH**-drah]
  - esquina
    [ess-**KEE**-nah]
  - este
    [**ESS**-tay]

  OR
  - oriente
    [oh-**REE+ENN**-tay]
  - carretera
    [kah-rray-**TAY**-rah]
  - cerca de
    [**SAIR**-kah/ day]
  - al lado de
    [ahl/ **LAH**-doh/ day]
  - norte
    [**NOR**-tay]
  - a la izquierda
    [ah/ lah/ ees-**KEE+AIR**-dah]

Appendix F:
Giving Directions (cont.)

- on the right
  - a la derecha
    [ah/ lah/ day-**RAY**-chah]
- red light
  - luz roja
    [**LOOSE**/ **RROH**-hah]
  - <u>OR</u>
  - semáforo
    [say-**MAH**-foh-roh]
- south
  - sur
    [**SOOR**]
- stop sign
  - alto
    [**AHL**-toh]
  - <u>OR</u>
  - pare
    [**PAH**-ray]
- stoplight
  - luz roja
    [**LOOSE**/ **RROH**-hah]
  - <u>OR</u>
  - semáforo
    [say-**MAH**-foh-roh]
- straight ahead
  - de frente
    [day/ **FRAIN**-tay]
  - <u>OR</u>
  - derecho
    [day-**RAY**-choh]
- street
  - calle
    [**KAH**-yay]
- to the left
  - a la izquierda
    [ah/ lah/ ees-**KEE+AIR**-dah]
- to the right
  - a la derecha
    [ah/ lah/ day-**RAY**-chah]
- traffic light
  - luz roja
    [**LOOSE**/ **RROH**-hah]
  - <u>OR</u>
  - semáforo
    [say-**MAH**-foh-roh]
- west
  - oeste
    [oh-**ESS**-tay]
  - <u>OR</u>
  - occidente
    [ohk-see-**DEN**-tay]

Appendix G:
Glossary

agreement | trato
[**TRAH**-toh]
OR
acuerdo
[ah-**KWAIR**-doh]

amount | cantidad
[kahn-tee-**DAHD**]

asking price | precio inicial
[**PRAY**-see+oh/ ee-nee-**SEE+AHL**]

attorney | abogado
[ah-boh-**GAH**-doh]

bargain, to | regatear
[rray-gah-tay-**ARE**]

black | negro
[**NAY**-groh]

block (city) | cuadra
[**KWAH**-drah]

blue | azul
[ah-**SOOL**]

blue, dark | azul marino
[ah-**SOOL**/ mah-**REE**-noh]

blue, light | azul claro
[ah-**SOOL**/ **KLAH**-roh]

bronze | bronce
[**BROHN**-say]

brown | café
[kah-**FAY**]
OR
marrón
[mah-**RROHN**]

building code regulations | reglamentos de edificación
[rray-glah-**MEN**-tohs/ day/ ay-dee-fee-kah-**SEE+OHN**]

cable TV | televisión por cable
[tay-lay-vee-**SEE+OHN**/ por/ **KAH**-blay]

column | columna
[koh-**LOOM**-nah]

condition | condición
[cone-dee-**SEE+OHN**]

closing date | fecha de cierre
[**FAY**-chah/ day/ **SEE+AY**-rray]

deal | negocio
[nay-**GOH**-see+oh]

disclosure | declaración
[day-klah-rah-**SEE+OHN**]

due date | fecha de vencimiento
[**FAY**-chah/ day/ venn-see-**MEE+ENN**-toh]

easement | zona de servidumbre
[**SOH**-nah/ day/ sair-vee-**DOOM**-bray]

furniture | muebles
[**MWAY**-blays]

Appendix G:
Glossary (cont.)

gold (color)	dorado [doh-**RAH**-doh]
gray	gris [**GREESE**]
green	verde [**VAIR**-day]
market price	precio en el mercado [**PRAY**-see+oh/ enn/ ell/ mair- **KAH** -doh]
market value	valor en el mercado [vah-**LOHR**/ enn/ ell/ mair-**KAH**-doh]
mortgage	hipoteca [ee-poh-**TAY**-kah]
multi-colored	multicolores [mool-tee-koh-**LOH**-rays]
multiple listing service (MLS)	listado múltiple de casas en venta [lees-**TAH**-doh/ **MOOL**-tee-play/ day/ **KAH**-sahs/ enn/ **VENN**-tah]
orange	anaranjado [ah-nah-rahn-**HAH**-doh]
pink	rosa [**RROH**-sah] <u>OR</u> rosado [rroh-**SAH**-doh]
plumbing	plomería [ploh-may-**REE**-ah]
purchase	compra [**COMB**-prah]
purchase price	precio de compra [**PRAY**-see+oh/ day/ **COMB**-prah]
purple	morado [moh-**RAH**-doh]
real estate	bienes raíces [**BEE+AY**-nays/ rrah-**EE**-says]
red	rojo [**RROH**-hoh]
residence	residencia [rray-see-**DEN**-see+ah]
silver (color)	plateado [plah-tay-**AH**-doh]
two-toned	dos tonos [**DOHS**/ **TOH**-nohs]
warranty	garantía [gah-rahn-**TEE**-ah]
white	blanco [**BLAHN**-koh]
yellow	amarillo [ah-mah-**REE**-yoh]

Appendix H:
Property Features Checklist

Spanish [*English*]

Marque todo lo que se aplique o desee. [*Check everything applicable or desirable.*]

Ubicación [*Location*]

Ciudad [*City*]:_____

Vecindario/Barrio [*Neighborhood/Subdivision*]: _____

Cerca de un(a) [*Close to/Near a(n)*]:
____ escuela [*school*]
____ centro comercial [*mall*]
____ carretera [*highway*]
____ calle [*street*]
____ avenida [*avenue*]
____ tienda [*store*]
____ supermercado [*supermarket*]
____ parque [*park*]
____ parada de autobuses [*bus stop*]
____ parada del metro [*subway stop*]
____ otro [*other*]: _____

¿De cuál? [*Which one?*]:_____

General [*General*]

Precio entre $_____ y $_____. [*Price range between $___ and $___*]

Edad de la vivienda: _____ años. [*Age of property: _____ years old*]

Tamaño del lote: _____ por _____ pies. [*Size of the lot: _____ by _____ feet*]

Tamaño de la vivienda: _____ pies cuadrados. [*Size of the property: _____ square feet*]

Número de [*Number of*]:
____ personas [*people*]
____ niños [*children*]
____ plantas/pisos[*floors/stories*]
____ recámaras/cuartos [*bedrooms*]
____ baños [*bathrooms*]
____ automóviles [*automobiles*]

Características Exteriores [*Outside Features*]

____ vigilancia [*security guard*]
____ sistema de alarma [*alarm system*]
____ entrada vigilada [*monitored entrance*]
____ tejamanil de asfalto [*shingles*]
____ techo de metal [*metal roof*]

____ techo de teja [*tile roof*]
____ madera (pintada) [*(painted) wood*]
____ ladrillo [*brick*]
____ vinil [*vinyl siding*]
____ aluminio [*aluminum siding*]
____ garaje [*garage*]
____ cochera [*carport*]
____ vigilancia [*security guard*]
____ sistema de alarma [*alarm system*]
____ entrada vigilada [*monitored entrance*]
____ garaje [*garage*]
____ cochera [*carport*]
____ callejón [*alley*]
____ cuarto de lavado/lavandería [*laundry room*]
____ balcón [*balcony*]
____ pórtico frontal [*front porch*]
____ pórtico que da al sol [*sun porch*]
____ pórtico rodeado de tela metálica [*screen porch*]
____ terraza (cubierta) [*(covered) deck*]
____ cuarto de herramientas [*tool room*]
____ taller (con electricidad) [*shop (wired with electricity)*]
____ escaleras [*stairs*]
____ ventanas de vinil [*vinyl windows*]
____ ventanas con aislamiento [*insulated windows*]
____ ventanas de guillotina doble [*double hung windows*]
____ ventanas de guillotina sencilla [*single hung windows*]
____ ventanas de aluminio [*aluminum windows*]
____ banqueta/acera [*sidewalk*]
____ jardín [*yard*]
____ árboles [*trees*]
____ arbustos [*shrubs*]
____ pasto [*lawn*]
____ alberca/piscina [*pool*]
____ tanque séptico [*septic tank*]
____ planta de tratamiento de aguas negras [*treatment plant*]
____ bar [*bar*]
____ asador empotrado [*bar-b-que pit*]

Características Interiores [*Inside Features*]

____ cuarto extra [*bonus room*]
____ comedor (formal) [*(formal) dining room*]
____ sala [*living room*]
____ sala de estar [*family room/den*]
____ cuarto de juegos [*game room*]
____ cuarto de lavado [*laundry room*]
____ sótano [*basement*]
____ ático [*attic*]
____ oficina [*office*]
____ tragaluz [*skylight*]

Características Interiores [*Inside Features*](cont.)

____ escaleras [*stairs*]
____ cortinas [*drapes*]
____ persianas [*Venetian blinds*]
____ persianas de madera [*wood blinds*]
____ repisas empotradas [*built-in shelves*]
____ alfombra [*carpet*]
____ pisos de madera [*hardwood flooring*]
____ pisos de parquet [*parquet flooring*]
____ pisos de linóleo [*linoleum flooring*]
____ baldosas [*tile flooring*]
____ techo estilo catedral [*cathedral ceiling*]
____ closet para la ropa de cama [*linen closet*]
____ closet para los abrigos [*coat closet*]

Calefacción y Aire Acondicionado [*Heating and Cooling*]

____ calefacción central (de gas) [*central (gas) heating*]
____ calefacción de gas [*gas heating*]
____ calefacción eléctrica [*electric heating*]
____ chimenea [*wood burning fireplace*]
____ chimenea de gas [*gas burning fireplace*]
____ aire acondicionado central [*central air conditioning*]
____ unidades de aire acondicionado [*air conditioning units*]
____ aire acondicionado de gas [*gas air conditioning*]
____ aire acondicionado eléctrico [*electric air conditioning*]
____ unidades de aire acondicionado en las ventanas [*window units*]
____ abanicos de techo [*ceiling fans*]
____ calentador de agua de gas [*gas water heater*]
____ calentador de agua eléctrico [*electric water heater*]
____ calentadores de agua [*water heaters*]

Características de las Recámaras [*Bedrooms Features*]

____ vestidor [*walk-in closet*]
____ dos closets separados [*two separate closets*]
____ bathroom [*baño*]

Características de los Baños [*Bathrooms Features*]

____ regadera (separada) [*(separate) shower stall*]
____ tina [*bathtub*]
____ tina de masajes [*whirlpool*]
____ jacuzzi [*jacuzzi*]
____ dos lavamanos separados [*two separate sinks*]
____ ventana [*window*]
____ extractor de olores [*exhaust fan*]
____ gabinetes [*cabinets*]

____ vestidor [*walk-in closet*]
____ cerámica [*ceramic*]
____ porcelana [*porcelain*]
____ fibra de vidrio [*fiberglass*]
____ plástico [*plastic*]

Características de la Cochera/el Garaje [*Carport/Garage Features*]

____ puerta eléctrica [*electric door*]
____ repisas [*shelves*]
____ espacio para guardar cosas [*storage space*]

Características del Cuarto de Lavado [*Laundry Room Features*]

____ lavadora [*washer*]
____ secadora [*dryer*]
____ aire acondicionado [*air conditioner*]
____ gabinetes [*cabinets*]
____ espacio para un congelador [*freezer space*]

Características de la Cocina [*Kitchen Features*]

____ estufa [*stove*]
____ estufa sin horno [*stove top*]
____ estufa de gas [*gas range*]
____ estufa eléctrica [*electric range*]
____ horno empotrado [*built-in oven*]
____ horno separado [*separate oven*]
____ horno de gas [*gas oven*]
____ horno eléctrico [*electric oven*]
____ horno de microondas [*microwave oven*]
____ horno de microondas sobre la estufa [*over the range microwave*]
____ horno de microondas empotrado [*built-in microwave*]
____ lavaplatos [*dishwasher*]
____ refrigerador con congelador [*refrigerator with freezer*]
____ congelador separado [*separate freezer*]
____ fregadero doble [*double kitchen sink*]
____ superficie de Formica [*Formica countertops*]
____ superficie de baldosa [*tile countertops*]
____ superficie de mármol [*marble countertops*]
____ superficie de cerámica [*ceramic countertops*]
____ superficie de granito [*granite countertops*]
____ área para comer [*dining area*]
____ "isla" para trabajar en la cocina [*work island*]
____ alacena [*cabinet pantry*]
____ compactador de basura [*trash compactor*]
____ triturador de basura [*garbage disposal*]
____ máquina para hacer hielo [*ice maker*]
____ electrodomésticos (nuevos) [*(new) appliances*]

This front and back of this form may be reproduced and used as needed, but only by the buyer of this book, "Spanish for Real Estate."